THE DRAWINGS OF HOKUSAI

Self-portrait of Hokusai at the age of 62

葛飾の翁

THE DRAWINGS OF HOKUSAI

Full name: HOKUSAI KATSUSHIKA

BY THEODORE BOWIE

INDIANA UNIVERSITY PRESS | BLOOMINGTON

CONTENTS

ILLUSTRATIONS

FOREWORD

Hokusai is known to the West principally as a designer of color-prints, and his name is linked, even in the minds of those who know little else about Japanese art, with the great landscape series, the "Thirty-six Views of Fuji," the "Waterfalls," and "Bridges." Less known are his verve and dynamism as a draftsman with the brush, and in this book—the first to be devoted exclusively to Hokusai's drawings—Professor Bowie approaches the subject in an original way that is bound to interest all those who have any appreciation of the art of drawing.

Apart from introducing to the public for the first time many splendid works, he deals in a rational and uncommitted way with the problem that has always confronted the student of Hokusai's drawings, and many who are more casually interested: the absence of a canon of works generally accepted as the artist's own incontrovertible brushwork. The difficulty of authentification is due to a variety of reasons—the uncritical because uninformed acceptance, in the early days of enthusiasm for Japanese art, of almost any Japanese drawing that had somehow acquired the label of Hokusai, either by misunderstanding, or the machinations of dealers; the difficulty of detaching these old labels; the system, in the Japan of Hokusai's day, of authorized copying of a master's drawings; the adeptness of pupils in adopting their master's style; the practice of copying book-prints when re-issue became necessary and the old blocks were worn out. By a study of many hundreds of drawings and of his printed works in broadsheet or book form as well as the more widely accepted *kakemono,* it is possible, I think, to develop an accord, an empathy, with the artist, so that any drawing truly from his hand is recognizable, like the voice and accent of an intimate. The author, over a long period of years, has acquainted himself with multitudes of Hokusai and quasi-Hokusai drawings; one senses his rapport with the artist and this gives us confidence in his judgment.

Of course, no empirical method of authentification such as this is ever likely to enjoy universal acceptance, and there are a few drawings over which I, for one, might join issue with the author, but by-and-large, the drawings he has selected for illustration do represent very fully the many-sided genius of Hokusai as draftsman and go a long way to establish, in an accessible and compact form, the anthology of characteristic drawings of the master that has hitherto been lacking.

JACK HILLIER
Redhill, 1963

PRELIMINARY NOTES

THE ILLUSTRATIONS

WITH the exception of the work reproduced in figure 116, which is presumed lost, I have examined all the drawings discussed in this study at first hand. Those which are indicated as belonging to various dealers may have passed into other hands. Mr. Tikotin gave the bulk of his collection to the Museum of Japanese Art in Haifa, a circumstance which made it difficult for me to check the dimensions of the drawings he kindly allowed me to photograph for use; these dimensions are consequently omitted.

As used here, the word drawing applies to a variety of productions, from extremely rough sketches on flimsy paper to detailed and finished works. It includes cutters' transparencies which have survived simply because they were never used, copying or study sheets with sketches on two or three sides of the page for the supposed use of several pupils simultaneously, water-color washes in red with corrections in black, and others, less hasty, with added tones; finally, some very carefully drafted line drawings which were conceivably prepared for presentation to friends or for sale to admirers. Although Hokusai is reputed to have been very catholic in his use of implements, all the drawings appear to have been done with the conventional brushes in India ink *(sumi)*. Corrections sometimes occur in the form of snippets of thin paper pasted over a detail. The papers used vary considerably in size and quality. As preserved by dealers, collectors, and museums, the drawings exist either as mounted or unmounted items, separately or in albums, handscrolls or screens. Where the sketches are intended to illustrate a book they often occur in the format and dimensions of the intended volume.

Hokusai's reputation as a draftsman was very great in Japan during his lifetime. His friends and collaborators prevailed upon him to publish various sketches and compositions in a number of miscellanies, such as the *Manga* or *Gashiki*. In republishing them in modern editions for the American and European markets, publishers have given them titles (such as the "Sketchbooks" of Hokusai) which suggest that original drawings are involved. This is not the case; these publications reproduce woodcuts of originals which have all disappeared, whereas the present work presents mainly original drawings, with a small number of woodcuts introduced solely for purposes of comparison.

SPELLINGS

Inconsistencies in the spelling of Japanese names and titles are the result of different systems of transliteration from the Japanese into European languages. An attempt at uniformity has been made in the case of these most frequently used words:

Hokusai is sometimes rendered as Hok'sai, which is the way the Japanese pronounce the name. French variants include Hokousai, Hokousaï and Hoksaï.

Manga is preferred over the older *Mangwa*. The word *gwa* (or *ga*), meaning sketch or drawing, appears in such composites as *Gwashiki, Gwafu, Sogwa,* etc., which are now written *Gashiki,* etc.

Ukiyo-e appears sometimes as *Ukio-ye* or *Ukiyo-ye.*

Yehon, or illustrated book, is now usually rendered as *Ehon.*

Various books illustrating the One Hundred and Eight Heroes, an extremely popular subject, use the title *Shimpen Suikoden,* or *Shimpen Suiko Gwa Den,* or *Shinpen Sui Ga Den.*

JAPANESE SCHOOLS OF PAINTING

Hokusai is considered to be one of the great masters of the *Ukiyo-e* school of painters, which flourished in the seventeenth and eighteenth centuries. It is commonly held that the school declined after his death in 1849. The term *Ukiyo-e* is often rendered as

"The Floating World," though some critics believe that "The Fleeting World" is a more correct rendering. Either way the term alludes to the fugitive and unstable character of the passing show which these artists portrayed. Many of them are better known to us for their prints rather than their paintings, though there is no essential difference in style and subject matter between these two forms. This subject matter included first of all the life of the theatre and of the pleasure quarters in the big cities, the delights of domestic occupations among the wealthy bourgeoisie, the daily activities of the popular classes, and the natural beauties of Japan.

Such stress on local and national themes was in the pure Japanese tradition developed in the thirteenth and fourteenth centuries by the artists of the *Yamato-e* or Art of Japan school, familiar to us mainly though their *makimono* or narrative scrolls. The tradition was maintained in the sixteenth and seventeenth centuries by the members of the Tosa school, while the opposite tendency of a return to the Chinese examples, particularly those of the Sung period, was fostered by the artists of the Kano group and their latter-day followers who are sometimes referred to as the "Classicists." Actually there are no hard and fast lines which separate the many movements discernible in Japanese painting. An eclectic, Hokusai was intensely familiar with all these currents and reflected them in turn or blended them to suit his purposes.

Introduction

My original purpose in presenting a book of drawings by Hokusai was simple: I wanted to acquaint
the student, the layman, and the collector with the rich variety of
work—sketches, drafts, preparatory materials, fugitive and spon-
taneous statements—left by one of the world's great draftsmen, well
known to us through his prints and book illustrations, less so
through his paintings, and very insufficiently through his drawings.
In the process of gathering suitable examples, however, I found
that I had to solve two basic, interrelated and inescapable problems postulated by the abundance of available material: how to
determine its authenticity, and how to date it with some hope of
accuracy. I therefore resolved to make myself familiar with as much
of Hokusai's total *oeuvre* as was humanly possible; and I devised a
rudimentary method of stylistic analysis to supply an objective
basis for inevitably subjective judgments.

In the course of a career that lasted more than seventy years,
Hokusai is thought to have composed 40,000 to 50,000 pictures.
There is nothing improbable in these figures if we add to all of his
paintings, prints, and book illustrations the thousands of drawings
attributed to him that are found in museums and collections all
around the world. I have had the opportunity of examining a number of them at first hand, and of accumulating a large photographic
file of them; I must make clear at once that my search was anything
but exhaustive. The majority of the drawings reproduced here
have never been published before, but I have used familiar ones
as well.

The preservation of huge quantities of drawings by (or ascribed to) Hokusai is natural, as outside of Japan he was long considered the greatest as well as the most representative Japanese artist. Beginning in the latter part of the nineteenth century, European dealers, following the example of Hayashi and S. Bing,[1] literally cleaned out Japan of all items that might conceivably have had some connection with Hokusai, with two results: it is almost impossible today to find original drawings by him in Japan (those that were not exported undoubtedly perished in the natural and man-made calamities to which Tokyo has been periodically subjected); and European and American museums and private collections were flooded with works of highly uneven quality, all more or less indiscriminately attributed to a single artist.

As Western knowledge of Japanese art increased and deepened, Hokusai was toppled from his eminence and eventually relegated to minor rank. His prodigious productivity could not be denied, but there was evidence that he had had many helping hands; skepticism, particularly in connection with his drawings, replaced faith. *Hokusai?* or *School of Hokusai?* began to appear on labels of works exhibited. In short, Hokusai as a draftsman became a highly controversial subject.

The complex task of authenticating Hokusai's drawings involved more than merely artistic considerations. In his book, *Graphic Art of Japan*, O. E. Holloway presents an argument against even trying.[2] In the course of a brilliant study of a neglected group of Japanese draftsmen of the so-called Classical School (Bumpō, Gesshō, Baitei, Suiseki among others), he states his case with unnecessary venom. It will be useful to refute his objections one by one.

ONE The making of wood-block prints for single sheets or for book illustrations is a collaborative process occurring in three separate states: the preparation of the design, the cutting of the block, the printing. No state is more important than any of the others, and while a competent man can perform all three operations, they require so much time that his production would be disastrously limited in a situation requiring mass production. The cutter and the printer become highly trained specialists who make a valuable contribution to the work in process; it is only artistic snobbishness which causes their names to be forgotten and the full credit assigned to the designer. The latter's original sketches are only a means to an end and therefore relatively negligible.

If we accepted this argument we would be saying that none of the great printmakers—Harunobu, Utamaro, Sharaku, Hiroshige, Hokusai, or any other in a long list—had a clear idea of what they intended to accomplish; that they depended on others to fulfill their intentions, and had little control over the results. Without denying the possibility of fortuitous changes, happy or otherwise, caused by the need for extra hands, we cannot explain the development of a personal style and the uniformity of artistic expressiveness to be found in all of the artists without accepting the primacy of the artist-designer, who prevails to the degree that he can resist encroachments—many of them commercially motivated—on his integrity as a creator. Far from being negligible, original sketches, provided they are authentic, offer valuable clues to the quality of an artist's inspiration and a check on his ultimate vision.

Because of the enormous demand for his designs and illustrations Hokusai was forced to set up a series of workshops and to train a number of assistants to work in his manner. These assistants, subject to his constant supervision, were collaborators in a truer sense than were his cutters and printers; the latter were more likely to be beholden to his publishers than to the artist himself and frequently worked at an inconvenient distance. We know the names of many of these helpers and something of their work independently of their connection with the master, and we know that some of them were highly talented. What we do not know with absolute certainty is what they were called upon to do. Did they prepare final work sketches and cutters' transparencies only, or were they allowed to submit original ideas and eventually to develop them, subject to the master's corrections? This problem is not so insoluble as it may at first seem; it has engaged the attention of various European and Japanese scholars.

TWO   Hokusai's fame has been so great that it has tended not only to obscure the merits of other artists, but has also given luster to anything, good, bad, and indifferent, that might be ascribed to him, and a false value to the merest scrap or studio sweeping that might be attributed to him.

The first part of this objection was never valid in Japan and is no longer valid in the West. An important distinction must be made between Hokusai's reputation in his own country and his fame abroad. He became extremely popular in Japan about 1810 and never ceased to be so, but only among the lower middle classes. Even today, when the entire Japanese attitude toward prints has changed from scorn to admiration, Hokusai is still regarded as "vulgar" and inferior to Harunobu and Utamaro. As for his fame in Europe and America, much of it rests on that regard for realism and raciness so despised by adherents of an idealistic approach to art. In any case, Revon, writing more than sixty years ago, pointed out that the excessive admiration for Hokusai in the West rested on ignorance of Japanese art, and that time would reveal his true proportions, without diminishing his stature.[3] As for the last point, it is bootless to hold Hokusai up to obloquy for having been exploited, long after his death, by unenlightened critics or unscrupulous dealers.

THREE   What is more important, that a drawing be good, or that it be by someone in particular? If it is more important that the drawing be good, why bother trying to distinguish between the master's hand and those of competent assistants?

Precisely to counteract the tendency to ascribe all good drawings to Hokusai and all inferior ones to his assistants. Hokusai, like Homer, occasionally nods. But if we wish to see the master's true face, warts and all, we can learn from his faults as well as from his virtues. We do not debase Hokusai if we finally attribute a good drawing to one or another of his disciples; giving him credit to which he is not entitled is actually rendering him a disservice. Hence the importance of trying not only to distinguish between master and pupils, but among pupils as well. This latter task, undertaken by Hillier,[4] may not seem especially rewarding but it is nonetheless essential, primarily for one reason.

It is highly probable that, with very few exceptions, none of Hokusai's amanuenses ever thought that their work would pass for his. The confusion is not the result of conspiracy. There is only one documented case of a pupil so clever and talented, and so injudicious at the same time, as to forge Hokusai's signature and seal. The man, known as Katsushika Taito II, succeeded for a time in hoaxing the public, but he was denounced by Hokusai and exposed. He still bedevils us today, for while we are familiar with what Bokusen, Hoku-un, Gakutei, Hokkei, Isai, Shigenobu, and other followers of Hokusai produced on their own and can judge their comparative merits, Taito must remain indefinitely suspect until he can be fully isolated.

FOUR The originality of an idea is not so important as how it is developed; hence first or rough sketches, improvisations, and other such fugitive documents are of little significance.

A distinction must be made here between the originality of a theme or subject and the manner of treating it. It is a truism in art that there are no original subjects. Like Shakespeare, Molière, or any other creative artist, Hokusai takes his wealth where he finds it. What is meaningful is what he does with it; therefore all the variations that his mind plays with a theme, his tentative decisions and his rejections, all the steps that illuminate the workings of his mind, are of value to the student. The world has come to treasure every scrap left behind by a genius, and to mourn the loss caused by a heedless disdain for the sweat and tears that creation entails.

FIVE Even if we succeeded in collecting only good drawings by Hokusai and in separating his work from that of all possible imitators, how can we ever be sure that we are looking at a work produced by the master's own hand and not at a very good copy?

This is a most difficult objection to rebut satisfactorily because of the peculiar status enjoyed by copies in Far-Eastern painting. The sixth principle of Hsieh Ho's celebrated Six Canons of Painting, enounced about the year 500, stresses the value of "transmitting the experience of the past by making copies." Observance of this doctrine has had two effects: we know something about ancient

art (painting in particular) which would have otherwise been totally lost; and copying has become an art in its own right. Now the
whole question turns on what is worth copying, not for the sake
of profiting from a forgery (although this is not necessarily a negligible motive) but to "transmit the experience of the past."

Good copying requires not only practiced skill but a scrupulous
attitude on the part of the copyist. He must render the flow of line,
the subtle turns and pressures of the brush, the luminosity of ink,
and all the other exacting imponderables which convey an artist's
intentions. These are very demanding requirements; we must ask
ourselves whether any drawing by Hokusai would have merited
such attention. He himself does not seem to have put his signature
and seal on more than an extraordinarily small number of drawings, but we assume that he did not disown all of the others which
do not have these signs of approval. We also suppose that he made
a number of sketches specifically intended to be copied by his pupils, and we suppose further that some of these copies were so good
as to obtain his approval. How far are we justified in thinking
that these facsimiles are good enough for our limited purpose,
which is to analyze his style? Presumably they lack that magic quality with which only the master's own hand can endow them, the
recognition of which cannot be tested in any valid, objective way
and which only self-appointed experts can identify. The dilemma
cannot be denied, but its importance should not be exaggerated.

SIX   Does not the work of art count less than the public for
which it was made?

No doubt about it, unless one implies that a work of art is the
anonymous emanation of a vague entity called "folk culture,"
"society," "the spirit of the times," or whatever. Art is the product
of an individual sufficiently sure of himself to give form, direction,
and meaning to life as he finds it; his public exists as an amorphous
and unselfconscious lump until he molds it. Hokusai holds up a
mirror to that aspect of nature with which he is familiar. Because
he is not a perfect artist, that mirror is not perfect, and we see in it
a slightly distorted picture of Japan of one hundred and fifty years
ago. But what his contemporaries in Japan saw they recognized as

a valid picture of themselves. Without wishing to use such misleading terms as "democratic" or "proletarian" with reference to him, we are well justified in calling him the poet of the common people of Japan. He is their most representative figure, and he never aimed at any other public. All we know about his life proves that he never tried to rise above his class, that of artisan-craftsman. And it is his drawings rather than all his other finished work that reveal his most intimate and immediate and vivid contacts with the source of his being.

The British Museum in 1948 observed the centenary of Hokusai's death in a notable exhibition of his works. This was followed by similar exhibitions all over the world, and by the publication of articles, monographs, general studies, and reproductions in facsimile of such works as the *Manga* and the *One Hundred Views of Japan*. Since then, the balance of critical judgment has been swinging back to increasing respect for Hokusai as an artist. His drawings have received enough attention, during all this activity, to indicate the need for critical studies from diverse angles. I am therefore encouraged to submit the results of my study at this time, in full awareness, of course, of their necessarily controversial nature.

Another encouraging fact is a purely personal one. I happened, early in my study of Hokusai, to read Jakob Rosenberg's little essay, *Rembrandt the Draughtsman*.[5] It was heartening to find that identical problems exist with reference to an artist who is vastly better documented than Hokusai will ever be, though he antedates him by two hundred years. Presumably the method employed to solve the riddles posed by the one might serve for the other.

Rosenberg suggests three criteria for determining the authenticity of a drawing by Rembrandt. The first is the judgment of experts and connoisseurs, subjected over the years to professional criticism; the next is a *consensus omnium*, or general agreement among all the experts; finally there is time. Through these tests, copies, compared with authentic drawings, tend to assume their proper place; attributions of pupils' work to the master are corrected, again by comparison with authentic drawings; finally, forgeries stand out nakedly when there is a corpus of authentic work by which to judge them.

It is precisely such a corpus of authentic drawings by Hokusai that I hope to establish. I have been guided by the descriptions of drawings left by Goncourt, Hayashi, and Fenollosa among others, and by the judgments of such experts as Mr. Kojiro Tomita, late Curator of Asiatic Art in the Boston Museum of Fine Arts, Mr. Harold P. Stern of the Freer Gallery, and Mr. Jack Hillier of London; the latter is also to be warmly thanked for writing a foreword. I record my indebtedness to them while absolving them of all responsibility for my own opinions. I also wish to acknowledge with deep appreciation the help given by Mr. Basil Gray of the British Museum, Mr. B. W. Robinson of the Victoria and Albert Museum, Mr. Alan Priest of the Metropolitan Museum of Art, Miss Margaret Gentles of the Art Institute of Chicago, Dr. Richard Fuller of the Seattle Museum of Art, Mr. Robert Treat Paine of the Museum of Fine Arts in Boston, and Mr. S. Kikuchi of the Tokyo National Museum, among others. The kindness of such collectors as MM. Harari of London, Louis-Léon Weill of Paris, and Robert Laurent of Bloomington in placing their holdings at my disposition must also be mentioned. And I am greatly obliged to Mademoiselle Marianne Densmore and Madame Huguette Berès of Paris, and to M. Felix Tikotin, formerly of Wassenaar and now of La Tour de Peilz in Switzerland, for the unrestricted use of Hokusai drawings in their possession.

A generous grant by the Research Committee of the Graduate Division of Indiana University enabled me to launch this study. In the final preparation of the text and illustrations I have received invaluable help from Miss Edith R. Greenburg and Mrs. Lou Ann Brower of the Indiana University Press, which I gratefully acknowledge.

T.B.

HOKUSAI'S STYLISTIC SHIFTS AFTER 1800

2. A *sake* bout.

ONE Katsushika Hokusai started illustrating books, under the name of Shunrō, about 1784. For the next fifteen years or so he worked in a variety of manners reflecting his easy adaptability to the styles of many artists he admired: Shunshō, Harunobu, Kiyonaga, Kōrin among others. By comparison with his own later works, these early efforts seem undistinguished. His soldiers, workers, and peasants have a stolid, not to say wooden, look about them; or, in violent contrast, other figures, especially his women, have a thin, elongated, and mannered stance. Mastery of composition is the only trait that he displays at all stages of his career. As far as can be determined, no original drawings from this early period have survived. Those who wish to see examples of his early styles may consult general books such as those of Hillier and Boller, which contain excellent reproductions.

About 1800, in his fortieth year, Hokusai seems to have experienced a sense of liberation; perhaps at this time "he found himself." The entire second, and major, part of his career shows a succession of experiments and stylistic shifts which are neither easy to relate to his first phase nor susceptible to study in terms of evolutionary or cyclical growth, fruition, and decay. Fenollosa analyzes them according to what we may call his Theory of the Five Manners. The first manner corresponds with the period 1800-1804 and is characterized by the drawing of elongated figures; the second, in the years from 1804-1813, is a "frank, vigorous and picturesque" phase; the third, from 1813 to 1826, is marked by a "lowering of standards, carelessness of line-feeling, exaggeration of action and pose, and the emergence of short, dumpy women." From 1826 to 1836 Hokusai reacts from this tendency toward "buffoonery"; he "hardens and purifies his line, achieving an exquisite touch." His final manner indicates both a return to violence of expression and a further suppression of the crisp line.[6] Boiled down to simple terms, Fenollosa's theory is one of alternation between a smooth, sinuous line and a broken one, sometimes even "crumbly," and between graceful forms expressing felicitous moods and violently distorted shapes betraying a fundamental vulgarity. As it betrays Fenollosa's prejudices, this analysis is too subjective to be very useful. It ignores the fact that Hokusai, like Picasso, is a centrifuge, throwing off styles from a perpetually rotating center of creative energy; that the birth of a new manner does not necessarily mean the death of any of the older ones; that an artist can work in several manners simultaneously; and that the demands of a given subject— as well as the artist's ceaseless and often expressed desire to improve himself—govern stylistic changes more directly than shifts in the quality of public taste.

The twenty-odd original drawings of all kinds presented in this chapter are intended to illustrate a corresponding number of styles and manners. The term "style" is used here to convey a general way of drawing, determined by subject matter (i.e., the "*Suikoden* style"), "manner" to describe either variation within a style or imitation of another artist, depending on the context. Differences between them are sometimes striking; at other times, there may be only a nuance, albeit a significant one. The chronological sequence must be somewhat arbitrary, since few of these drawings have a signature, seal, or other precise indication of a date. I have based my sequence on the dates of publication of the illustrated books, prints, and paintings with which I connect these drawings, even though these dates are not always reliable. Up to a certain point, for example, we can follow Hokusai's development throughout the publication of the fifteen volumes of his *Manga*, though we cannot be sure that the last three volumes reproduce drawings which belong uniformly to his last phase.[7] Sometimes there seems to have been a protracted delay between the preparation of a book and its

1. Five figures in mixed settings.

3. Sketch for an illustration for *Hidano Takumi Monagatari*.

actual publication. I have also avoided attempting to correlate any of his manners with such external events in his life as family troubles and illness. Hokusai, for instance, suffered from an attack of palsy which lasted from 1829 to 1831. It is tempting to explain some of his shifts in these terms, but it would be hazardous to do so in the absence of indisputable evidence. Finally, his own remarks to the effect that he had not really learned to draw until he was a very old man and wished that he could live to be 100 or 105 years old so that he could come to fruition may be accepted only as a sign of modesty.

The first sketch depicts a stormy, wintry scene. Its alternation between indoor and outdoor setting makes it somewhat ambiguous, though some kind of unifying element was probably intended. The brush stroke is nervous and sharp, and the patterns bold. Hillier suggests that this may be an illustration for a novel published around 1804, but offers no further clarification. The lines terminate in sharp wedges typical of that period; the sense of volume, weight, and texture of the woman's robes is well conveyed, and the two men conversing in the rain form an expressive group. *figure 1*

The drawing of three old, happy drinkers in different poses is either a presentation sheet or a teaching sheet. It may well have been done in a late period, but it is representative of the manner used by Hokusai around 1803, for example in the illustrations for *Jinkōki no Yurai*. This satirical book of mathematical precepts, burlesques a seventeenth-century work on arithmetic, the first written by a Japanese. The illustrations are characterized by bold strokes ending in upward wedges, exaggeration of muscles in arms and legs, and particular attention to fingers and toes. Variations on the poses are found in all subsequent phases of Hokusai's work; the resemblance in the figures and their attitude to those pictured here will be very strong. *figure 2*

A very detailed drawing, from the Metropolitan Museum's collection, is a study for an illustration in Volume 6 of *Hidano-Takumi Monagatori* ("The Craftsman of Hida," 1809-1810) by Rokujuyen. Its manner may be called transitional since the type of figure used here does not recur often in Hokusai's work. An *figure 3*

4. Carpenters.

opposite: 5. Tile-makers.

figure 4 over-all relationship in subject matter is evident in figures 4-7. The first three should perhaps be regarded as variants of one style. The first sketch, of carpenters at work, belongs to a set identified by Hillier as the "Occupations" series; it is dated 1811. This set was apparently never published, and there is no way of telling how many illustrations it was intended to have. The figures of the carpenters are not drawn with absolute sureness of line, and the calligraphic quality of the drapery has yet to be perfected. The figures, in their poses, features, and general expression, are beginning to look like the typical species of mankind that has been nicknamed *Homo Hokusaiensis;* the only thing lacking is the angular arm and leg muscles. Relationship of figures to background is introduced here, and in this respect the difference from the drawing for "The Craftsman of Hida" is striking. Now the figures are dominant and

7. Tooth-powder vender (water color wash in reddish and brown ochre tones).

6. Tooth-powder vender.

the setting is a background, instead of conversely. There is an interesting but undemonstrable possibility that Hokusai may, consciously or unconsciously, have been influenced by compositions in the Dutch manner, with which he became acquainted about this time.

figure 5 The effect of such a probable influence is more immediately evident in the TILE-MAKERS, which looks very much as if it were a part of the "Occupations" series. The landscape in the background, above the figures, can be said almost to have a vanishing point. The figures themselves are drawn with firmness and elegance; they are arranged in a pattern that is almost "manneristic." In their somewhat theatrical poses, they seem frequently to be aware of a public watching their performance. This is doubly curious: in the first place Hokusai is less interested in the theatre than almost any other *Ukiyo-e* artist. In the second place a great many of his figures, especially in his complex prints, are stereotypes, that is, they are drawn *de chic,* from memory. The initial observations on which they are based are apparently not renewed except occasionally, when there is a radical change of manner. How he manages to impart vitality to such stock types is a source of never-ceasing wonder.

figure 6 The TOOTH-POWDER VENDER is obviously related to the two previous drawings: an "occupation" is illustrated, and there is a stylistic connection. Yet there are some important differences: the line is sharper; the faces are more like those in the Hida sketch; and the bodies are becoming elongated. How much later is this sketch than that of the CARPENTERS? Possibly as much as fifteen years.

One very important clue to Hokusai's method is provided by this drawing: the two outlined forms to the left, and the third one on the right, suggest a habit of dealing in major patterns, which are broken into smaller ones; these furnish locations for figures, to be filled in eventually. In this respect the corollary habit of depending on a stock of stereotypes assumes its specific importance: the stock has to be immense as well as varied to be truly useful; and everything we know about Hokusai convinces us that this was the case.

figure 7 To us the figure of a man balancing himself on a post while wielding a long samurai sword in one hand and its sheath in the

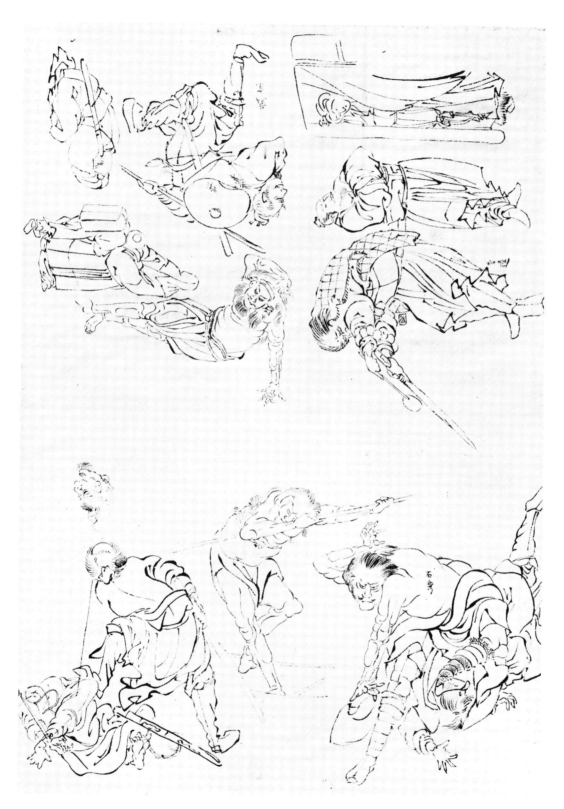

9. Study sheet of warriors.

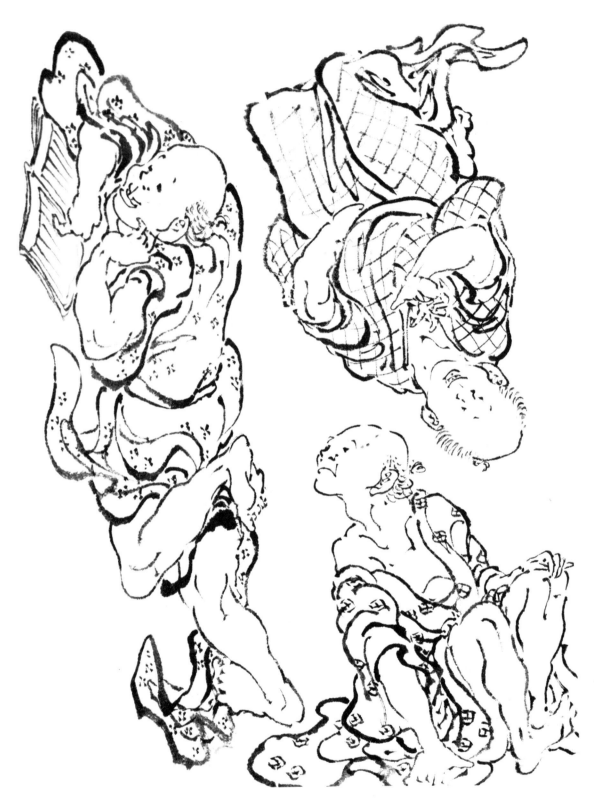

8. Miscellaneous men.

other may have warlike connotations; in Japan it was apparently the normal way for this vender to attract a crowd. We see the theme used in a page of the *Day and Night Sketches* (1819-1821). Even though these Sketches are closer to being water-color washes than drawings, we can easily see that the line here is so slack as to be called "crumbly." Yet this is only an apparent vice; there is so much vitality in this rough new style that it may indicate one of those occasions when Hokusai indulges in a wholly fresh set of observations and serves them, so to speak, piping hot; as essential form and movement are of primary importance in these sketches there is no preoccupation with nicety of line and an almost total elimination of facial features. Far from being a retrogression into vulgarity, the use of line here is a significant advance. This version of the TOOTH-POWDER VENDER is considerably more moving than its relatively arid predecessor.

The next sketch is a study sheet. Its loose caricatural manner *figure 8* relates it to the page of portraits and figures, from the same collection, dated about 1822, illustrated in figure 87. But looseness does not denote feebleness of touch or even carelessness; on the contrary, the figures in their various poses and in their expressiveness reveal great mastery of the brush and precise control of form. If caricature is intended here, it is reminiscent of Daumier.

Beginning about 1805 and continuing until his death, Hokusai was engaged in treating the multitudinous face of war. Histories, legends, and novels about Japan, China, and Korea, published to meet a ceaseless demand, required illustrations of which he was perhaps Japan's most prolific supplier. To take only one example among many: for the *Shimpen Suiko Gwa Den* ("Illustrated New Edition of *Suikoden*"), which came out in ninety volumes between 1805 and 1828, he provided 632 compositions. This kind of subject matter thus constituted a challenge to his inventiveness. It may also have brought him close to a very large public. Sober, industrious, and stoical, the Japanese people have a long martial tradition. Their history is particularly bloody; in Hokusai's lifetime, which corresponded with the relatively peaceful end of the Tokugawa regime, the memory of feudalism was not dead. In portraying legendary heroes and warriors, in describing their

11. Three personages from the *Suikoden* (enlarged detail of figure 104).

violent deeds with enormous gusto, he was therefore satisfying popular taste without necessarily being jingoistic. His best-known and probably most popular creations, the figures in the *Suikoden*, are Chinese, however. To invest these personages with authenticity he created forms and a general style which may be called "Chinese." Purists may point out all kinds of errors, but for general purposes the Chinese look is plausible enough. The terms "*Suikoden* style" or "Chinese style," as used here, refer to content and background rather than to the character of the drawing; variations, similar to those found in his treatment of other subjects, occur in this style. The four examples adduced here illustrate some of those variations; it is not possible to define the span of time they cover,

10. General Kwan Yü being bled.

opposite: 12. Ra-setsu-jo, Prince of the Iron Fan.

but I am inclined to think that they all fall within the years 1820-
1830, and that they are representative of that period. Hokusai
himself did not think very highly of his earliest work in this category; there is no doubt that it improved steadily as he went along,
and that the illustrations he did after 1835 have a force of expressiveness which is remarkable, despite his fairly florid handling of
the brush.

figure 9   The first example in this group is a three-sided copy sheet in the
Metropolitan Collection. Two of the *Suikoden* personages are
identified. The incisive stroke and the simplification of arm and
leg muscles into a series of angles are characteristic of Hokusai
from 1820 on. These drawings may have been preparatory to the
one-volume book of illustrations without text, portraying the One
Hundred and Eight Heroes of the *Suikoden* in characteristic situations and poses, and published in 1829.

figure 10   GENERAL KWAN YU BEING BLED WHILE CONTINUING TO PLAY CHESS
is a perfect blend of Chinese costumes and props with a type of human figure that according to Hokusai's conventions can also be
either Japanese or Korean. If we forget the staging and concentrate
on the situation, we can appreciate the profound psychological insight and wit in the artist's treatment of the subject.

figure 11   The next is a detail from a drawing fully illustrated in figure
104; the signature and the seal of this great but little known work
by Hokusai states that it was *Fusenkyo Tamekazu hitsu,* "done
by hand by Tamekazu," a name used by the artist about 1823.
Short strokes, ending in a wedge are blended with somewhat looser
and softer lines as if, in order to convey the mood of warriors at
rest, the artist has mingled the hard and soft in equal doses.

figure 12   The last example in this group represents the legendary char-

羅刹女
一名
鉄扇公子

acter called the PRINCE OF THE IRON FAN. The manner is definitely
baroque, both in the exaggerated *contrapposto* of the figure and
the abundance of wavy lines in the drapery. Indulgence in such
mannerisms, not unusual in earlier periods, is unusual for 1830,
tentatively assigned as the date of this drawing. Echos of this man-

figure 13   ner may perhaps be perceived in the next drawing, which is strikingly different in every way except for its rich brush stroke. This
representation of a man lying lazily dreaming and of a boy crouching at his right is also a masterpiece of psychological observation.
The subject and the pose are to be found in *Manga* XII (1834),
but the woodblock has none of the fine contrast between the lush

13. Summer *sake* sippers.

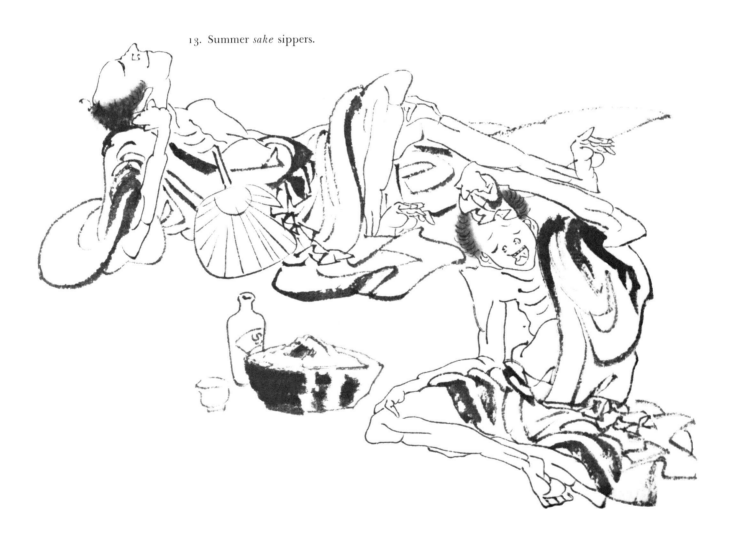

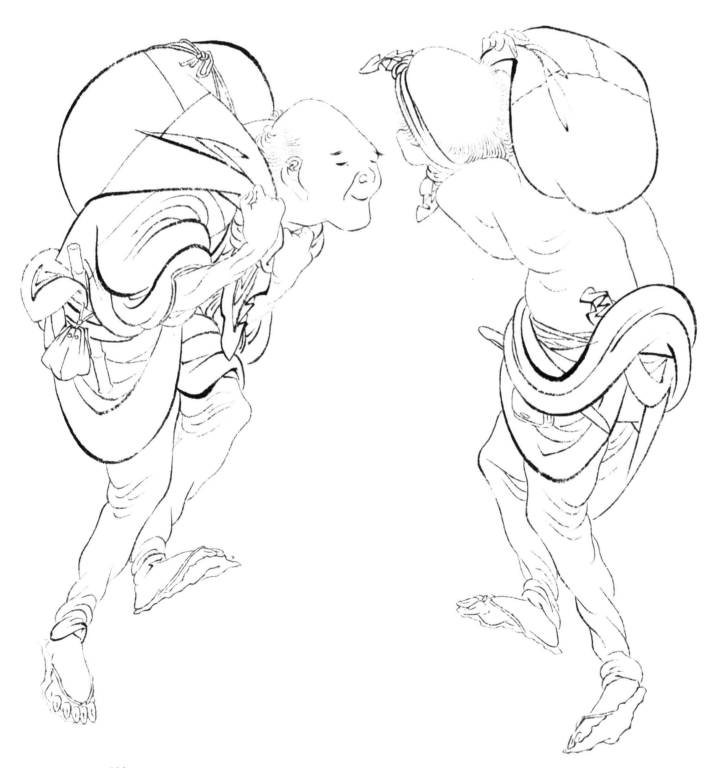

14. Old men carrying bags.

16. Preparations for a feast.

opposite: 15. Sheet of brush drawings.

treatment of the drapery and the thin, elongated arms and limbs. A companion drawing, showing two reclining women, appears in figure 76.

figure 14   Two OLD MEN CARRYING BAGS on their backs and passing each other on the road form the theme of a presentation drawing. The manner is a refinement of the preceding one and is representative of the 1830-1840 period, possibly Hokusai's high maturity. Yet the British Museum gives 1835-1840 as the date for another and very *figure 15*   different three-sided study sheet in its collection; the manner is more painterly (this term is perhaps more accurate than the word "loose"); in contrast to comparable manners, faces are detailed and facial expression is of prime importance.

The last two drawings are offered as examples of Hokusai's manner after 1840. The first one is a page from the final preparatory *figure 17*   sketches for the *Nisshin-Joma-chō* ("Book of Daily Exorcisms"), which was published in 1842-1843. It shows a lion-dancer wearing his heavy mask and holding his drum strapped around his neck, trying to open his umbrella in a heavy downpour. The book contains some sixty or seventy pages of illustrations that are handled with a rich and heavy brush. In the same spirit, but with greater *figure 16*   crispness, is a rough description of kitchen preparations. All the essential movements are indicated; facial features, except for the eyes, are missing in the actors, but the artist's intention, which is to give us the bustle and excitement pervading a kitchen at a crucial moment, is fully conveyed. If it is a sample of Hokusai's very late manner, it clearly indicates that his powers had not weakened with age.

opposite: 17. "March 28" (drawing for *Nisshin-Joma-chō*).

五
月
五
日

HOW HOKUSAI WORKED

49. Travelers.

TWO The variations of manner perceptible in Hokusai's drawings are less easily seen in his prints and illustrations, not because the woodblock is incapable of reproducing fine distinctions of brush-stroke but for crasser reasons. Like many of his fellow printmakers, Hokusai was somewhat at the mercy of his woodblock cutters, as well as his publishers. Even at the height of his fame he was not always able to obtain new effects in his reproductions, either because the technicians had established a standard look from which they were unwilling to depart or because the editors wanted no deviations from certain manners that had become popular and profitable. That editors were, on occasion, not above encouraging—or blinking at—the use of other artists' mannerisms is apparent in a letter written by Hokusai, begging them not to permit the use of Kuniyoshi's wrong method of doing eyes and noses.[8] A good drawing, whether it is rough or carefully *figure 91* worked out, tells us more about the creative processes of a draftsman than any print can, provided always that its authenticity can be established. It must not be forgotten, however, that such a drawing is only a step in the production of a finished work; rarely is it ever an end in itself—exceptions, in Hokusai's case, are those very smooth and polished sketches that we assume to have been drawn for presentation purposes.

In the course of studying various collections and assembling a corpus of photographs, I have come upon different kinds of

越後大鮹
又夢

18. The giant octopus of Echigo (rough sketch).

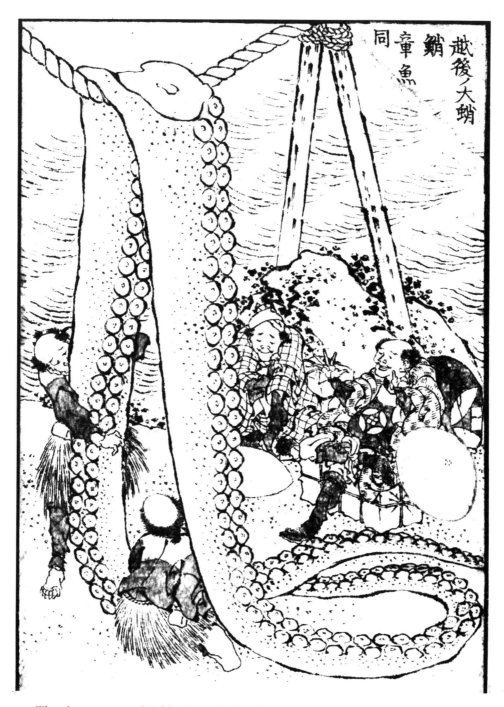

19. The giant octopus of Echigo (cutter's sketch).

20. Taisō (working sketch with *pentimenti* in red).

21. Taisō (cutter's sketch).

22. Taisō (detail of figure 9).

23. Procession of monks before an altar (rough sketch).

sketches, in widely separated places, that seemed to have an organic relation to one another. In the same way, I have found others unmistakably connected with a print, an illustration, or a painting, or all three. In a sense such comparisons are implied throughout the body of this study; this chapter, however, is entirely devoted to the problem of these relationships through a detailed series of analyses in terms of technique, figure types, composition, and thematic developments.

FROM ROUGH SKETCH TO FINISHED WORK

A cutter is normally supplied with a clearly outlined, detailed drawing on transparent paper, which he pastes face down on his

24. Procession of monks (illustration in *Ehon Tekin Orai*).

block and which is intended to guide his knife. As this tracing is doomed to disappear, we might dub the method the "lost-paper" process, by analogy with the lost-wax process in bronze casting. It is axiomatic that any cutter's drawing that reaches us has not fulfilled its destiny. Fortunately for the student, a number of such specialized sketches still exist, either singly or bound in books. Some of them are obviously copies of books for use in future editions; it must be remembered that woodblocks erode very rapidly after a few score pressings. Work that exists only in the form of cutters' tracings is therefore doubly interesting.

Along with these specialized tracings the designer may also provide the cutter, and eventually the printer when there is color to be applied, with fuller sketches or cartoons, sometimes in color, at other times merely with color indications. (Detailed cartoons were presumably not needed in the case of a new edition, unless the artist wished to change his composition.) Hokusai provides us with a wide variety of these guiding sketches, some reflecting lavish care in preparation, others having been hastily corrected with superimposed bits of paper. At times a given work will appear to have had numerous preparatory sketches and at others the concept, the development, and final corrections will all be seen on the same sheet. It is not always easy to tell a *première pensée,* as Goncourt called Hokusai's rough sketches, from his afterthoughts; sometimes his red lines mean corrections; at other times they cannot indicate anything but first drafts.

Did Hokusai create all these different kinds of sketches with his own hand? Is his touch at all perceptible if assistants were used?

25. Man bowing before altar (rough sketch).

Such assistance is more than probable in view of the enormous number of illustrations he undertook to produce; it is unlikely in the case of his paintings, which did not require the service of amanuenses. The validity of the answer will depend on how clearly the evidence submitted below can be interpreted.

Hokusai was undeniably capable of providing a complete set of sketches for his engravings; he had had professional training as a cutter and, in theory at least, he was well qualified to fulfill three-fourths of the job of the *Ukiyo-e* quartet[9]: artist, cutter, and printer. (He evidently did not have enough interest or business sense to be a publisher.) We will never know whether any engraved

26. Man bowing before altar (illustration in *Ehon Tōshi Sen*).

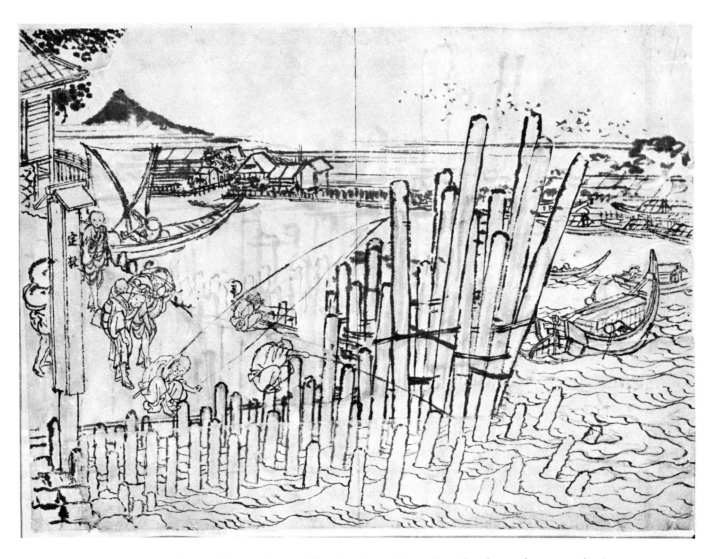

27. View of Mount Fuji from Shimada Bay (working drawing with *pentimenti* and pasted-on corrections).

28. View of Mount Fuji from Shimada Bay (illustration in *Fugaku Hyakkei*).

work was entirely produced by him; we only know that the cir-
cumstances of his life and the conventions of his craft make this
improbable.

We may also take for granted that he relied on his own ideas
and worked out his sketches himself; he clearly did not have to
depend on outside inspiration, which is not to say that he would
refuse suggestions from outside sources. He had such insight, such
an ability to see the implications of a subject, that even when he
borrowed a theme from some contemporary he could always go
further and deeper with it.

This stage, when sketch passes on to engraving, presents the greatest problem. The only pair of drawings uniting a rough or preparatory sketch with a cutter's sketch that I have found is the group
figure 18 dealing with THE GIANT OCTOPUS OF ECHIGO. They have identical
dimensions. As there is no known print of this subject, those who
figure 19 would criticize the rough drawing on the ground of weakness—
implying that it is not by Hokusai's hand—might have to argue
that it had been copied from the cutters' sketch—which is fairly
implausible. The figures in the cutters' sketch are typical of his
middle period; it is interesting to see their transformation from the
more individual personalities in the first sketch to a standardized
figure type. The seated man who is throwing his arms up in admiration is not unlike many figures we encounter in the drawings
of various periods, and the man next to him also crouches in a
characteristic attitude. Their counterparts occur a thousand times
in the prints and books of the artist. If we assume that this cutters'
sheet was prepared by an assistant, there is every reason to suppose
that it was accepted and approved by Hokusai, who may well have
made some corrections in his own hand. There are numerous evidences of similar corrections in this collection of unused cutters'
sketches, and in others that have come down to us.

The group of drawings connected with the illustrations of the
single-volume edition of the "One Hundred and Eight Heroes of
the *Suikoden*" is more complex. The British Museum possesses an
album of fifty-three working sketches for the *Ehon Suikoden*, published in 1829. They are described as "in sanguine and ink, with
pentimenti, and fuller indications of landscape than in the wood-

29. Study of eighteen men in different poses.

31. Twilight scene of Mount Hira in the snow.

30. Illustration for a novel (rough sketch in red ink with *pentimenti* in black).

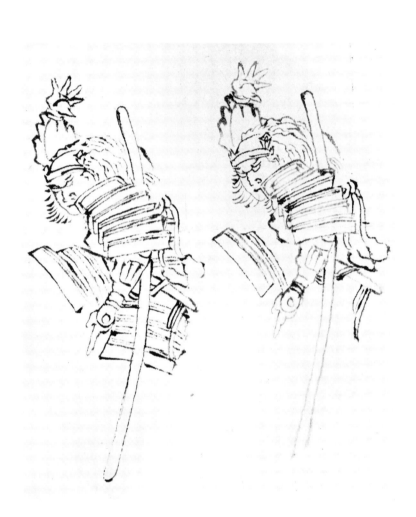

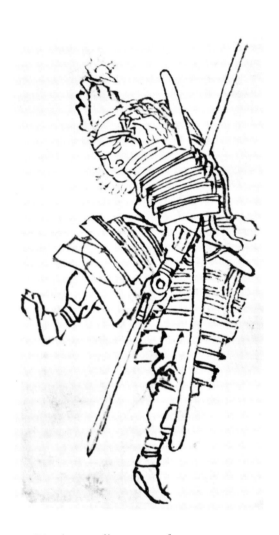

35. Two warriors, with legs not drawn.

34. Warrior standing on one foot.

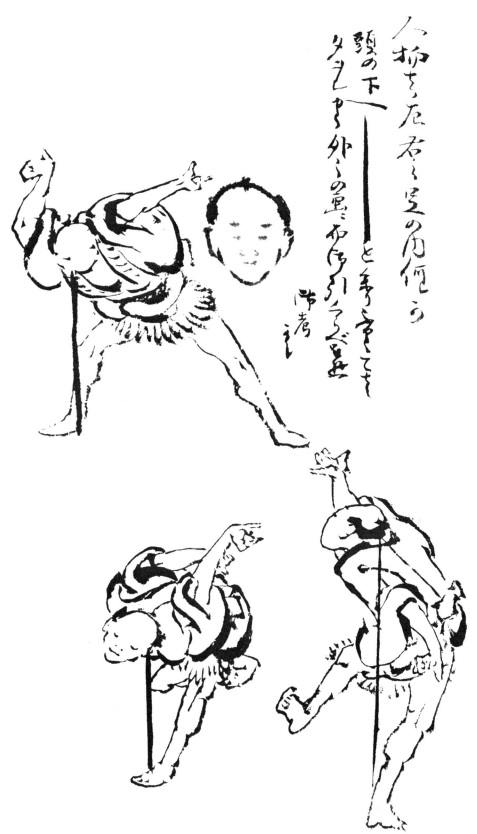

32. Yakko in three poses.

33. Warrior poised to strike.

figure 20

cut." For present purposes I shall consider a single page, but my observations are applicable to the entire set. The page I have chosen represents the personage named TAISŌ. This hero is always shown running: the Law of Divine Discipline requires that he travel 1,600 miles every day. By comparing the working sketch with the woodblock illustration in any of the numerous editions enjoyed by the work, one can feel confident that the British Museum owns an original set of drawings. But is this the actual first draft? The Metropolitan owns a three-sided students' sheet in which Taisō is represented and identified for us; there are many significant differences, however. Two contradictory conclusions are possible concerning these drawings: the latter drawing represents afterthoughts, and typifies the artist's desire to refresh a theme that has become hackneyed by constant reiteration; or it is a first version. I am inclined to adopt the second view. In figure 22 Taisō *figure 22* is shown in full profile; his torso swings from left to right, though his legs are in the same general position as in the later drawing. Finally there is not very much of a Chinese look to this member of a famous Chinese band. Vigorous as its movement may be, this personage is less interesting psychologically than the standard Taisō, whose face is shown in three-quarter view, resting on the cushion formed by the well-padded sleeves of his upraised arms, a gesture which also protects it from the wind.

The Boston Museum owns a complete set of cutters' sketches *figure 21* for this special volume of illustrations from the *Suikoden* minus the text of the novel. In spite of differences of detail (costumes, backgrounds, and labeling) these sketches are very close to the British Museum set of working drawings. What we will never be able to know with any certainty is how many sets of cutters' transparencies were made. Anywhere from two hundred to a thousand prints could be made from one set of blocks. Nor can we guess the moment when a new edition was ordered by the publishers. Would the cutters' sketches be made from the original drawings, or (what is more probable) would they have been prepared from a good copy of the printed book? The part that Hokusai himself played in controlling the re-edition of an extremely popular work of his is also a matter of speculation. It is highly possible that his publishers did not consult him, but it is also logical to suppose that they would try to maintain fidelity to an accepted and recognizable style.

Three preparatory sketches unmistakably related to published *figure 23* works give a good idea of Hokusai's methods of composition during the latter part of his career. The first represents a group of priests *figure 24* participating in a religious ceremony. The drawing is used to illustrate a page of *Ehon Tekin Orai* ("Communication of Home Precepts," 1828). The pictures in this book offer indirect com-

36. Dancer with lion mask.

37. Buddhist divinity (water-color wash in black and red from the *Jukkan-shō* scroll).

mentary on the text rather than pictorial interpretation. In the drawing there is little differentiation among the figures; their features are reduced to a minimum; in the woodblock the handling of details tends to individualize these figures.

The next pair of examples also illustrates a scene with religious or ritualistic overtones, though the number of participants is sharply reduced. We are dealing here with an illustration for *Ehon Toshisen*, a collection of poems of the T'ang period with comments by the Japanese poet Takai Ranzan; it is the fifth picture in the first volume, published in 1836. Here the brush is looser and freer than in the previous drawing; the sketch has some elements of a watercolor wash. It shows more qualities of an early version than the preceding example: the final book illustration has lost the personage standing to the left and gained three others crouching in prayer around the table. The central figure remains in essentially the same pose, but the sense of deep veneration, humility, or supplication conveyed by the final version is lacking in the sketch, where the man merely seems to be making an obeisance to a superior. Originally, also, the scene is placed outdoors, though there is a certain ambiguity about the framed doorway to the right.

The preparatory sketch for the "View of Mount Fuji from Shimada Bay," which is found in Volume 2 of *Fugaku Hyakkei* ("The Hundred Views of Fuji"), dated 1834, shows a high degree of correlation with the final version, while combining in itself the features of a first, second, and revised draft. Both the sketch and the engraving have identical dimensions, taking into account the fact that the format and size of the book would demand the splitting of the composition into two vertical halves, each to be engraved separately. In the sketch we can perceive the original layer on which the first idea was lightly drawn in red ink. (Successive phases of completion are evident from the bits of thin paper pasted over the first sketch.) The next stage was the firm organization of the scene, almost as if it were a stage set: pier, piles, houses, boats, and Fuji off in the distance. An area in center left remained free to be filled in with figures. Here it becomes very clear that, in his later period at least, Hokusai used the "cutout" system. Every one of the figures, crouching fishermen, men and women standing or

figure 25

figure 26

figure 27

figure 28

38. "Mad Poet" (detail from a sheet with other figures).

39. High wind dispersing the revelers at the Gion Festival (unused drawing in the *Hyakunin Isshū* series).

walking, singly or in groups, is a standard item in his repertory. In different sizes and proportions these individuals, with identical poses and movements, appear hundreds of times elsewhere. In an arrangement of this kind their general location is plotted out in advance; they may be drawn in at an early stage, or a spot may be saved for them, as is clear from the fact that two standing figures are missing in the sketch. The thin bits of paper on which they were drawn have simply been lost. A cutter's sketch could easily be traced from this one, and trained cutters and printers accustomed to Hokusai's manner would not really need further guidance.

Hokusai's habit of preparing a repertory of people in closely
related poses is exemplified in a sheet which gives some fifteen   *figure 29*
poses of a man moving and gesturing in pugnacious attitudes;
there are back views, side views, three-quarter views, almost as in
a stop-motion series. How much the artist depended on direct
notation and how much on memory it is hard to say; if these
sketches were made without a model they rest on a very solid base
of early observations.

But the artist did not always compose in a mechanical manner.
At times he would proceed organically, by making people and
background part of a cohesive design, as the various drawings
collected in this book amply prove. The following two examples
turn specifically to this point. The first, a very rough sketch for-   *figure 30*
merly in the Hayashi Collection, is in preparation for a double-
page illustration, probably of a novel that has not been identified.
The men and the background were very clearly drawn in red;
those on the right side remain uncorrected; the two men in the
left half show the red lines under the black. This method is dic-
tated by the needs of the story illustrated.

In the drawing labeled TWILIGHT SCENE OF MOUNT HIRA IN THE   *figure 31*
SNOW the mountain and the expanse of air and water between
the foreground and the background fill most of the composition.
Inconspicuously, there are six human figures in the lower right
and a boat being poled on the left. They are obviously not afterthoughts; they all seem necessary, though minor, concomitants of
the scene. We cannot say as much for the figures in the drawing
of Shimada Bay above; there we have a kind of stage set, and the
number of personages walking on the pier could be decreased from
ten to six or fewer without spoiling the composition.

EQUILIBRIUM, TENSION, AND MOTION
AS MAJOR THEMES

Hokusai is one of the great celebrators of the Japanese landscape;
he is also famous for his animals and his flowers. Yet he probably
did many more studies—of unequal quality—of the human form in

40. Shōjō, a drunkard proving his strength (water-color wash).

五雜　豊年

藏入　登歳

倉同

廩庫

41. Strong man holding up a bale of rice (cutter's sketch).

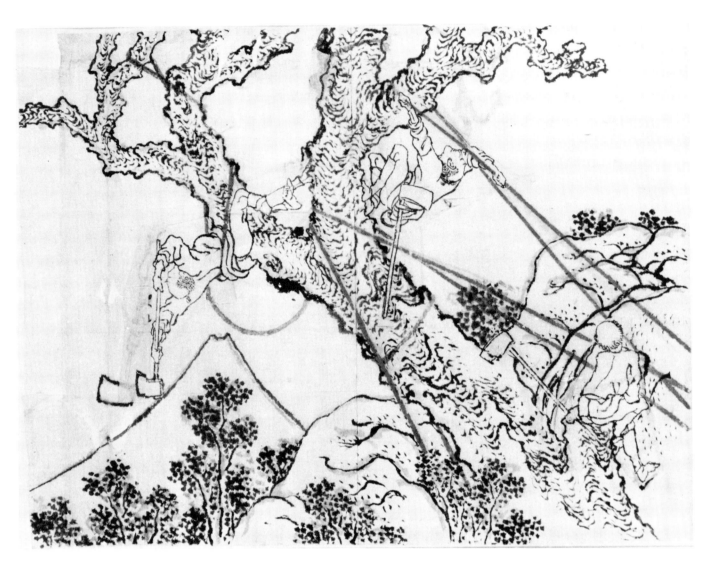

42. Woodcutters (working drawing with *pentimenti* and corrections for an illustration in *Fugaku Hyakkei*).

opposite, above: 43. Rope-winders (unused drawing in the *Hyakunin Isshū* series).

below: 44. Rope-winders (cutter's sketch).

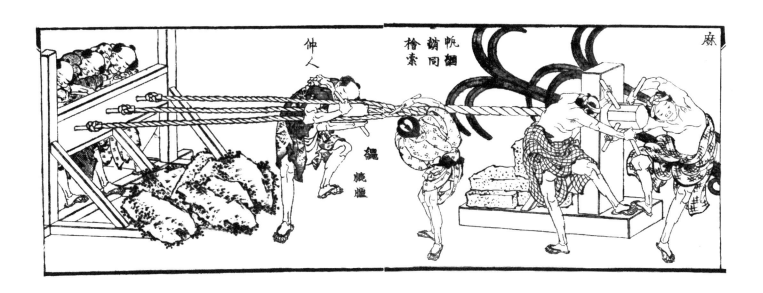

45. Wrestlers (drawing with *pentimenti* in black over red).

every conceivable attitude: in war, play, at work, in the dance, in ceremonies, indoors, outdoors, clothed, partly clothed, or naked, at all ages and belonging to all social levels except the aristocratic. He wanted to express the pulsating vitality of a human being under given conditions of stress, as both his rough and more finished sketches make clear.

The drawings in this section show humans in a state of equilibrium, often associated with one or another form of dancing; in a state of tension caused by a struggle with matter or against other humans; and, finally, in motion, either across the page, or toward or away from the viewer.

figure 32 The sheet entitled YAKKO IN THREE POSES illustrates the proposition that "in drawing a human figure, if either the right or left foot is not in a straight line below the head, he will fall down."

The artist accordingly draws a heavy black line connecting the upper part of the body with the extremities. Hokusai used such a device in *Odori Hitori Geiko* ("Dancing Self-taught") published in 1819. It is not clear whether he was enunciating a general truth or describing a particular stance, because he is not consistent in applying the principle. Correctly interpreted it means that the head should be in line with whichever foot supports the weight of the body. The principle is followed in the sketch of the bearded warrior who, holding one foot up in the air, is about to bring down a heavy weapon on an adversary.

figure 33

This principle is also illustrated in the drawing of a warrior in a bellicose stance, which is echoed twice in another sketch; here the missing legs suggest that Hokusai draws his figures from the head down instead of from the ground up. The seeming formality of this pose is reminiscent of a religious performance and may be seen in the wash drawing of a lion-dancer. There the performer holds the heavy mask over his left shoulder with his right arm while working a fan with his left hand. The same kind of equilibrium is achieved by the man holding the dough in the MOCHI-MAKERS illustrated in figure 53, and in related drawings. Whether the performer stands on his right or left foot, all other parts of his body move rhythmically to assure his balance. If he is holding a heavy object or wielding a weapon, the distribution of weight is nicely calculated. It is interesting to compare these studies with an iconographic drawing, dated 1142, of the divinity Ashura standing on his left foot with six of his eight arms brandishing various symbols. The source of this work can be traced back through China to India; it could have served as a sketch for a painting or a piece of sculpture, and it raises the hitherto unexplored topic of Hokusai's indebtedness to the traditional forms of Buddhistic art, especially in their Japanese aspect.

figure 34

figure 35

figure 36

figure 37

The most striking example of managed equilibrium is to be found in the figure of the so-called MAD POET. The character for "Wind" appears at the right, as it does in a comparable double page in *Manga* XII. The artist has not followed his own precept regarding the relation of head to feet, but no matter how disarticulated the man seems to be, he is not going to lose his balance.

figure 38

Drunk, ecstatic, or mad, here is the very spirit of the wind, un-predictable and fantastic but not uncontrollable.

figure 39 Resistance to wind is the theme of a drawing interpreting a poem by Bunya-Yasumaro (a name also read as Bun'ya no Yasu-hide). A sudden storm disrupts the preparations for a festival, and the participants react in strained but harmonious attitudes. Hoku-sai also likes to express resistance to stress in terms of a strong man—worker, farmer, or wrestler. He is usually shown from the *figure 40* back, in the act of holding at arm's length a bale of rice weighing *figure 41* 131 pounds. The weight is always supported through a violent haunching of one hip, the unused arm acting as a buttress on the small of the back. There is always a slight hint of mockery on the artist's part at the display of braggadoccio involved.

figure 42 Resistance to gravity is well illustrated in the working sketch for an illustration in the "View of Mount Fuji from Mount O-Mi" (in *Fugaku Hyakkei*). Here again the action of the WOODCUTTERS in bracing themselves upside down by means of ropes against the limbs of a tall tree while getting ready to swing a heavy axe is depicted as much for its implication of technical virtuosity as for *figure 43* its exhibitionistic element. The moving of huge inert masses is the theme of a finished drawing and of a cutters' sketch, the osten-*figure 44* sible subject in both cases being rope-making, which requires mul-tiple effort clearly dependent on rhythmic motion; the former drawing illustrates a classic poem to the effect that "life is like a rope which is equally woven with happy and unhappy strands."

Resistance to an equal force that one might expect to overcome through some species of mental calculation is the essence of wrest-ling. In *Sumo*, or Japanese wrestling, particularly, brain rapidly *figure 45* prevails over brawn. In one study Hokusai has caught that brief moment when the opponents, locked in an embrace somewhat reminiscent of a formal dance, seem to be perfectly matched; their twist to the left is balanced by the movement of the referee to the right. A similar example of motion arrested in time is perceptible in the sketch of THE ARREST OF KIDOMARU (figure 115), described in detail later in this section.

Finally, resistance to natural elements—in this case in a literary *figure 46* context—is depicted in the sketch of the hero SABURO-NO-ISE fight-

伊勢三郎
大物の難

帆綱

46. Saburo no Ise (cutter's sketch).

ing against a storm at sea and trying with the energy of despair to
lash himself to a mast. The bulge of the hapless man's muscles
directly contrasts with the surge of the great waves.

Motion is an illusion that Hokusai is eminently capable of con-
veying through figures walking across, diagonally, and up and down
the page; they move away from or toward the spectator, singly or
in groups. The artist is equally skillful in rendering other more
dramatic kinds of human motion—dancing, climbing, jumping,
and swimming. Men in the simple act of walking challenge him
to exercise his power of psychological insight as humans reveal
figure 47 themselves as fully by their carriage as by the sound of their
voices or their manner of verbal expression. The FIREMEN, who

48. Lion dancers and musicians.

march in procession carrying their decorated pole to a festival, are intent on pressing on and quite ignore the inquisitive peddler and the *geta'ed* lady in their path. In a drawing that enlarges upon a theme used in *Manga* V, in the *Day and Night Sketches* and several other works, we see three *shishi dancers* proudly wearing their lions' manes and beating their drums, while their humbler and more prosaic fife-players follow at a respectful distance. In another drawing, the young and the old TRAVELERS, passing each other on the road, convey a meaning beyond that of an accidental encounter.

figure 48

figure 49

Another drawing from the series of the "One Hundred Tales Told by the Nurse" has for its subject the chasing away of spirits on Cleansing Day; the bent old man who carries a lantern as he walks away from the shrine manages to look both meek and skeptical. If, as some believe, this is Hokusai himself at the age of eighty, it is an appealing self-portrait. Walking in the opposite direction is a young woman carrying a lantern; her modest demeanor is in sharp contrast with the swishing carriage of the young woman in another drawing. She too is seen from the back, but her pride of place is unmistakable. Finally, we see a gentleman of Old Japan walking away from us, tootling on his fife with the most elegant unconcern: the loose lines with which he is drawn merely heighten his casualness.

figure 50

figure 51

figure 52

FROM THEME TO SUBJECT-MATTER: THE ''MOCHI-MAKERS''

The MOCHI-MAKERS, or Rice-Cake Pounders, a drawing in the collection of the Metropolitan Museum, is particularly suitable for stylistic analysis. The subject has often been treated by Hokusai; its theme is susceptible of diverse interpretations. Renditions of the same theme by other artists afford useful comparisons; and the drawing is closely related to one painting and at least one woodblock. We may therefore study it in a broad context.

figure 53

In *Things Japanese,* Chamberlain refers to the popular myth of "a hare in the moon, which keeps pounding away at rice in a mortar to make into cakes. The idea of the hare is borrowed from China, but the rice-cakes seem to be native, and to have their origin in a pun,—the same word *mochi* happening to have two acceptions of rice-cakes and full moon."[10]

It should be said at once that Hokusai appears to have neglected the theme of the hare and the broadly allegorical implications of the subject. The making of rice-cakes was traditionally part of the preparations for the Festival of the Full Moon in Autumn. Today it seems to have been shifted to the period around the first of January. Rice-cakes, or rather semi-circular flat-bottomed loaves, are a standard feature of the New Year's Festivities, but it is doubtful whether very many are made on farms. Even in Hokusai's time, it was recognized that the pounding of rice into malleable but sticky dough in a barrel-like mortar made out of a hollowed-out tree trunk is a dull and back-breaking business. Still, as a *genre* subject, *mochi*-making had poetic and festive connotations; the artist might also choose to stress the skill required for a proper performance of the operation, or else to make fun of the clumsiness of tyro's attempts. As a communal activity, at least two men were normally required, the pounder and the handler of the dough (though in *Manga* XI Hokusai depicts a mechanical pounder which eliminates one of the performers). Very often there is an audience whose participation is anything but passive. Before analyzing the drawing, let us examine seven other interpretations—three realistic, two poetic, and two satirical.

figure 54   The composition in *Manga* I (1814) fills a space no larger than three inches by five, but it gives us the essentials of the operation with a minimum of staging: one man finishing the downward stroke of his heavy mallet, the other poised on one foot with his arms full of the dough which he has just managed to lift before the incidence of the stroke, and two seated observers, one apparently still terrified by the central figure's narrow escape from being battered, the other clearly admiring the agility of the escape; to the rear left is an oven. In this brief compass Hokusai has given us a situation in which the performers act in a manner comparable to a ritualistic dance. The tension of hard work is present, but even more there is the exhilaration of coordinated motion before an audience that reacts strongly. The engraver has followed the quick strokes of the artist without trying to refine them, so that

47. Firemen proceeding to their Festival.

51. Walking woman.

there is a caricatural air, characteristic of many of the figures in *Manga* I, which should, however, not be misunderstood. In harmony with a very ancient tradition of Japanese art, Hokusai's peasants and farmers are drawn in a manner which seems comical to the Western eye. We must not infer from this that Hokusai thought them ridiculous—his satire is normally very explicit; this drawing is clearly not as satirical as some of the others in this series. Finally, while this is probably not his first treatment of this theme, all subsequent ones appear to be derived from it. The composition

50. Shinto priest exorcising a gateway (unused drawing in *Hyakunin Isshū* series).

54. *Mochi*-makers (illustration in *Manga* I).

of our Metropolitan Museum drawing is almost precisely a reverse image of this one.

figure 55   The second work is a much larger as well as more elaborate double page from Volume 1 of *Hokusai Gashiki,* published some five years after *Manga* I. There are five watchers now instead of three, but the two actors and the oven are in the same relative position as in the *Manga* I engraving. The cutter took great pains with his work and in good editions the color does not blur the sharpness of the brush-stroke, although we perceive an inevitable tendency toward angularity in rendering bodily features, the arm especially. The mood of the picture is good-humored, not to say festive, and while the watchers are participating with excited gestures there is no hint that they are joking about the principals.

Volume 2 of *Ehon Hayabiki* ("Picture Book of Quick References," 1819), a pictorial dictionary, illustrates with human or animal forms various words based on the *hiragana* syllabary. On this

53. The *Mochi*-makers.

55. *Mochi*-makers (illustration in *Hokusai Gashiki*).

page we see the basic sound equivalent to our broad *A* pictured by   *figure 56*
the word *awamochi*, which means millet cake. Although this is not
precisely making rice-cakes, the effort required is identical. We
see a pounder and a kneader working in a mortar and a third man
holding a basket. All three are faceless (the individual figures in
this book are much too small for details); the artist concentrates
on essentials. Muscular tension is one of them, and the artisans'
need to pay close watch so that a relatively hard and dangerous
job may be carried out efficiently. Hokusai's economy of statement
matches the carefully calculated motions of his actors. There may,
however, be some doubt as to whether the wielder of the mallet is
standing far enough away to prevent his next downward stroke
from overshooting the target.

    The same criticism applies to the earliest of the poetic treat-   *figure 57*
ments of the subject that can be discovered. This composition,

right: 57. *Mochi*-makers (illustration in *Ogura Hyakku Donsaku Kassen*).

56. *Awamochi*-makers (illustration in *Ehon Hayabiki*).

from *Ogura Hyakku Donsaku Kassen* ("Parodies of the One Hundred Poets," 1803) illustrates a *haiku* by Shunehōshi on the pensive poet's mood heightened (or disturbed?) by the sound of the neighbors pounding rice.

figure 58   The large-scale, fully worked out drawing illustrates a poem by a "high-ranking official of the Court," celebrating the preparation of the Autumn Festival under a clear full moon. The scene is laid on the banks of the Sumida River; two large mortars are set on straw mats, and two men are alternately pounding their mallets into each mortar. To the left a weary worker washes his feet in

58. Preparations for the Autumn Festival (unused drawing in the *Hyakunin Isshū* series).

59. The *Mochi*-makers (painting).

opposite, above: 61. *Mochi*-makers (print by Tōrin).

below: 62. *Mochi*-makers (illustration by Shigemasa).

60. *Mochi*-makers (illustration in *Manga* XII).

the river, and above him a youth carrying a torch leads a blind man off. The men who normally knead and pull up the dough are absent, nor is there any sign of an oven. None of the men wielding a mallet looks as if he had aimed carefully or was about to do so. We must infer from this that a sharp twisting of the handle occurs as the conical pestle is brought down; the illusion that lack of proper distance from the mortar might cause an accident exists even in modern photographs of the situation. Hokusai is therefore not guilty of faulty observation. In any event, here he is primarily interested in stressing the mood of the activity, its poetic and associative values; he takes special care in reproducing graphically the sounds associated with the work, emphasizing the rhythmic pounding of the mallets. The faults here, if any, occur not in the composition but in the exaggerated forms and attitudes of the pounders, all of whom belong to a human species that occurs, as many commentators have noted, only in Hokusai's late works, particularly distinguished by the almost baroque arabesques described by their clothing.

There is a Japanese proverb that says something like "Why bother making rice cakes when you can buy them at the bakery?" The implication is that amateurs can only make a mess of a job best left to the professionals. The consequences of disregarding this plain bit of common sense are depicted by Hokusai in two different media—one a painting and the other an engraving—done ten years apart, but strikingly similar in composition. The painting is *figure 59* signed Tamekazu, which would place it around 1823-1824. It illustrates a *haiku* by the nineteenth-century poet Hinamaro: "Younger will the face look with the arrival of the New Year, but its chin is now stolen by the mirror." This is one of those nearly unfathomable puns which Tomita interprets as follows: "The man, who is shaping the *mochi* dough into a round 'mirror' cake, is laughing so hard that his chin disappears at the sight of the mass of dough stuck to the pestle which is being raised by the pounder." This is exactly the subject of the *Manga* XII engraving of 1834, though *figure 60* there are three instead of four participants, and the onlooker appears irritated rather than amused.

Our central topic, the Metropolitan Museum drawing, is a very *figure 53* spirited composition; it represents Hokusai at his best. The idea sketched in miniature in *Manga* I (figure 54) is fully developed here, and its organization is more cohesive than the *Gashiki* composition (figure 55). Hillier considers the drawing a preparatory sketch for this woodblock, but I am inclined to disagree, on the ground that its tone has much more satire than the *Gashiki* illustrations generally evince.[11] It seems to me much closer in spirit to both the painting (figure 59) and the *Manga* XII plate (figure 60). The wielder of the pestle is clearly darting a furious glance at his work-mate, who is obviously dismayed. The attitude of the onlookers on the left is unmistakably derisive. As an illustration of the dictum that incompetents should not tackle *mochi*-making it far surpasses in subtlety the painting and the last engraving, both of which tend toward caricature. The drawing is perfectly balanced in mood as well as in design.

As none of the treatments by Hokusai of this subject of the *mochi*-makers antedates the year 1814, one may wonder whether he was familiar with two versions by older artists, with whom he

figure 61

was undoubtedly acquainted. The version by Tōrin was executed in 1796. Tōrin Tsutsumi was one of a group of artists clustering around Utamaro; he is remembered as the teacher of Shunsen, and he may consequently have also taught Hokusai at one time. The subject is handled in a decidedly matter-of-fact manner; his principal actors lack all sense of drama, and their spectators are singularly passive. The print has some limited documentary interest, but as a composition it is too pallid to have had much influence on Hokusai.

figure 62

By contrast Shigemasa's treatment looks as if it might have been a direct ancestor of at least one of Hokusai's versions. It occurs in the third volume of *Ehon Azuma Karage* ("The Tucking-up of the Garments of Eastern Men"), which is dated 1786. Kitao Shigemasa illustrated numerous books, collaborated with Shunshō in the making of some famous prints, and taught several generations of printmakers. His general approach to his subjects combines realism, humor, and poetic feeling, and in many ways he anticipated Hokusai as an interpreter of the Japanese scene. Compared with Hokusai however, he looks almost like a primitive. His rendering of the *mochi*-makers has the same type of farmhouse setting as Hokusai's in the *Gashiki*; there is the same sense of excitement, and the same concentration on the center of interest, which is the pounding—all this in contrast with Tōrin's diffuseness and the dismal attitudes of his people. But comparing these two early works with Hokusai's only serves to point up the latter's vigor and imaginativeness. There is no such thing in Far-Eastern art as an untouched subject, anymore than there is in Western art. Hokusai's originality obviously resides in his fresh, lively, and energetic approach to traditional topics, and in the variety of manners he can summon to this end.

MEN AND WOMEN AS HOKUSAI'S PRINCIPAL SUBJECTS

In stating that energy in its several manifestations, particularly balance, stress, and motion, was the central *theme* in Hokusai's art,

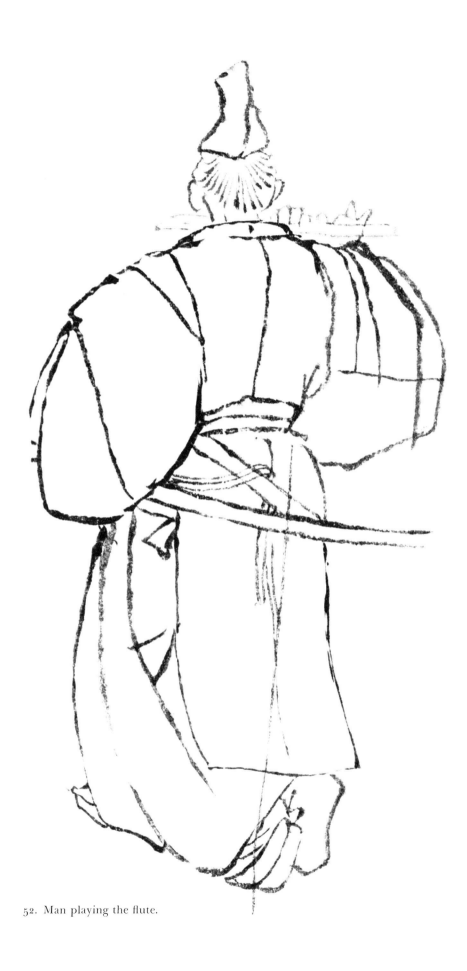

52. Man playing the flute.

63. Laughing men (detail from a sheet of miscellaneous drawings, see figure 106).

64. Summer relaxation.

66. The story-teller.

67. Gentleman being served.

69. The vender of New Year's poems (detail from the "Mad Poet" sheet).

68. Three musicians.

I indicated, at least by implication, that his preferred forms were men and women. In saying that his fellow countrymen were likewise his main *subjects* I am being consistent, as I am making the usual distinction between theme and subject. Theme is immanent, fundamental, and of the essence, while subject is transitory, local, and surface. In other words, the study of Hokusai's theme should tell us something of his people as human beings, whereas his handling of subject should tell us something about them as Japanese. This section is therefore devoted to Hokusai's view of his contemporaries. Without forcing terminology, one might say that in theme he operates as psychologist and in subject as sociologist, and perhaps also poet. As an observer of the Japanese scene, whether his attitude be that of a detached reporter or a sardonic commentator or critic, one can call him a realist in the same sense that the word is used in the West. But as an illustrator of historical novels— an occupation that preempted a very large part of his creative energies—he endows all his historical scenes and actors, whom he handled no less realistically than his other, more prosaic, *genre* subjects, with an imaginative quality that irresistably suggests a

65. Two lazy men.

romanticism akin to its Western counterpart. A man wielding an axe will use the same instrument and perform identical motions as the warrior or hero, but the difference will go much deeper than a change of costume. The grander figure will be surrounded by a heroic aura and the special atmosphere that the artist conveys so well, which immediately transports the scene from the everyday world into a special world of the imagination. For this reason then the drawings presented below are separated into two major, and obvious, categories. As usual, exceptions occur which make this division less than rigid.

The Realistic Approach

Among the surviving drawings of men there seems to be a preponderance of middle-aged and elderly figures—the younger men being found mainly in the warrior category. In his portrayal of women, although he does not neglect aged crones, Hokusai seems to prefer younger and prettier representatives of the sex, whether thin or fat. The majority of his drawings of children are of boys. The models generally belong to the middle or lower classes, since Hokusai had more opportunities for observing servants, artisans, tradesmen, farmers, and fisherfolk than more highly placed individuals. His sympathies seemed to lie with the common people even when he caricatured them. His mockery had no cutting edge.

Here is a group of drawings of men done in a variety of manners. In the first (one-half of a two-sided copy sheet) two crouching men *figure 63* laugh uproariously and gesticulate expansively. The brushline is fairly rich and the figures balance each other well; details of hands, legs, and feet are carefully handled, while the faces have that flat-nosed simplification that is one of Hokusai's trademarks. Alternating thin and thick lines distinguish the next sketch: two men, *figure 64* seated on the ground, are relaxing, their heads up. Both are partly unclothed; we are given here the rare opportunity of seeing how Hokusai handles the entire body at rest. The upper figure may be compared with that of the man on the left in the upper group of the British Museum version of the so-called MAD POET. The brush *figure 65* treatment here, although rougher, is essentially the same as in the

previous sketch. The attitudes of both the lounger and the man
reading occur, with little change, throughout a large number of
illustrations—the differences reside mainly in the character of the
brush stroke. The man seated on a low stool may perhaps be inter-   *figure 66*
preted as a STORYTELLER. His relaxed position and the upward tilt
of his head relate him to the figures just noted, but the style—
with its rapid but crumbly line, which is nevertheless expressive—   *figure 67*
suggests that it may be dated around 1840. The drawing of a gentleman at a feast receiving a platter of food from an unseen server
shows similar execution of line. The skill with which all the essential details in this vignette stand out make it a miniature masterpiece: the whole atmosphere of the feast is conveyed seemingly
without effort.

One attractive group of THREE MUSICIANS shows three men wear-   *figure 68*
ing identical costumes, vaguely Chinese; one plays a kind of fife

71. Woman in her tub being showered with gold coins (illustration in *Kamado
Shōgun Kanryaku-no-Maki*).

70. Crouching nude woman.

72. Woman powdering herself (print signed by Sōri).

while the others blow on their flutes. The seated figure on the right, seen from the back, is a close mate to several others, particularly to the walking man in figure 52.

figure 69

The VENDER OF NEW YEAR'S POEMS, from the Paris version of the MAD POET,[12] also relaxes sitting on a rock in a casual attitude, with one knee up. This elderly man wears the attire of a Shintō priest; a bow which he holds is strung with strips of paper. The inscription on this drawing, probably in Hokusai's own hand, reads: "*Utauru*, which originated with a Shintō minister of the Watari family." *Utauru* is telling fortunes by picking one of the slips on which are written poems; Watari is the name of an old family associated with the Ise Shrine, going back to the early history of Japan. A formal version of this subject in a painting is owned by the British Museum, but it has no specific connection with our drawing.[13]

Neither the male nor the female human body has been used as a vehicle for esthetic doctrines of perfection of form in Far-Eastern art. Consequently, the many partially dressed, undressed, and naked men and women in Hokusai's work do not carry any special connotation except when they occur in a freely erotic context. In the latter case a totally nude figure may often be less titillating than

figure 70

a partially disrobed one. The only sketch of a totally nude woman which I have found shows a squatting young woman scratching her armpit. She recalls the Danaë-like figure of the courtesan in *Ka-*

figure 71

mado Shōgun Kanryaku-no-Maki ("The Tactics of General Oven," 1800), who is showered with coins as she sits in her tub; a similar

figure 72

figure type, partly nude, was used in a print signed Sōri.[14] This woman, who is applying *araiko* (or cleansing powder) to her neck, and the other examples, with their informal gestures and their sensuous slightly plump bodies, recall figures found in *Manga* IV of around 1820.

figure 73

The heavy-set woman, nude from the waist up, in the act of adjusting her hair, is seen from the back in three-quarter view. The

opposite: 73. Woman adjusting her hair.

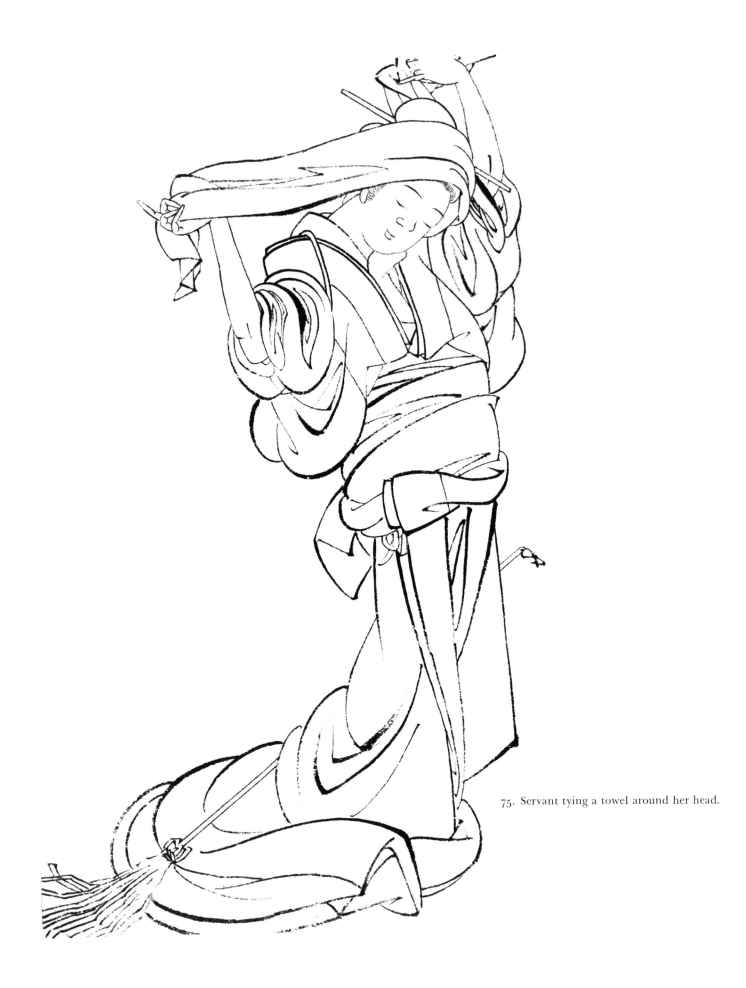

75. Servant tying a towel around her head.

line is vigorous, but the figure lacks that refinement of the form
found in such works as the next example. A plump young woman, *figure 74*
viewed from the front in this case, crouches on the floor while holding her mirror with one hand. She is found, in context, in the lower
lefthand corner of the British Museum version of the MAD POET.
The SERVANT TYING A TOWEL AROUND HER HEAD has all the careful *figure 75*
execution that we find in Hokusai's presentation drawings. The
wonderfully controlled arabesque is achieved by the calligraphic
handling of the drapery; there is a curious discrepancy between the
delicacy of the woman's hands and the coarseness of her face. Contrast this drawing with the next one done in a manner clearly related to that of the two men illustrated earlier (figure 13): TWO *figure 76*
WOMEN LYING PRONE on their stomachs, one reading and the other
drawing. There is more than a hint of the caricatural in the way
their limbs are drawn, but the handling of the brush in depicting

74. Woman crouching before a mirror (detail from "Mad Poet" sheet).

76. Two women lying prone (water-color wash).

the drapery is masterful. Yet how far they are from the elegant samisen players found in *Koppō Fujin Atsumi* ("Collection of Women in Hokusai's Structural Brushwork," 1822)! The woman playing the samisen in a rough sketch is clearly a first state for the woodblock, though we can see a tremendous elaboration in the calligraphic treatment of the drapery in the finished plate. Whether the next drawing is an intermediate working sketch cannot be exactly determined, but since the book was published posthumously—some fifty years after the drawings were made—there is a possibility that this is one of the finished sketches made by the artist himself to guide the printer. It is less probably a late copy because it would have had to have been made from the posthumous woodblock print, not a very likely event; nor is it a tracing, since the drawing is substantially larger than the book illustration.

figure 77

figure 78
figure 79

Finally there is the sketch of a woman in the embrace of an octopus. Full of *pentimenti*, it is clearly related to the famous erotic print, so eloquently described by Goncourt: ". . . that terrifying picture: on rocks made green by seaweed, the naked body of a woman, faint with pleasure, *sicut cadaver*, so much so that it is impossible to tell whether she is alive or drowned, and whose lower parts are being sucked by an enormous squid with its frightening eyes like black moons, while a smaller squid greedily devours her mouth."[15] The myth illustrated here tells of a fisherwoman, married to an unsatisfactory husband, who dreams of the all-enveloping embrace of an octopus. In the drawing the woman reclines in an only half-recumbent position; she is not completely nude, nor is she more than half-asleep. Her head and her expression are reminiscent of the woman in THE RAPE, and although the location of the squid's head may conform with logic, it is far less powerfully erotic than in the print. This presumably is the earliest version of the work, and far inferior to it.

figure 80

figure 81

figure 116

That there should be relatively many more sketches of boys than of girls in Hokusai's work may merely be the reflection of a popular rather than personal attitude. Certainly in his own life his daughters showed more filial piety toward him than his sons. The little boys shown at play in this handful of sketches from various sources are drawn with humor and tenderness.

*figures
82 to 86*

77. Samisen player (rough sketch).

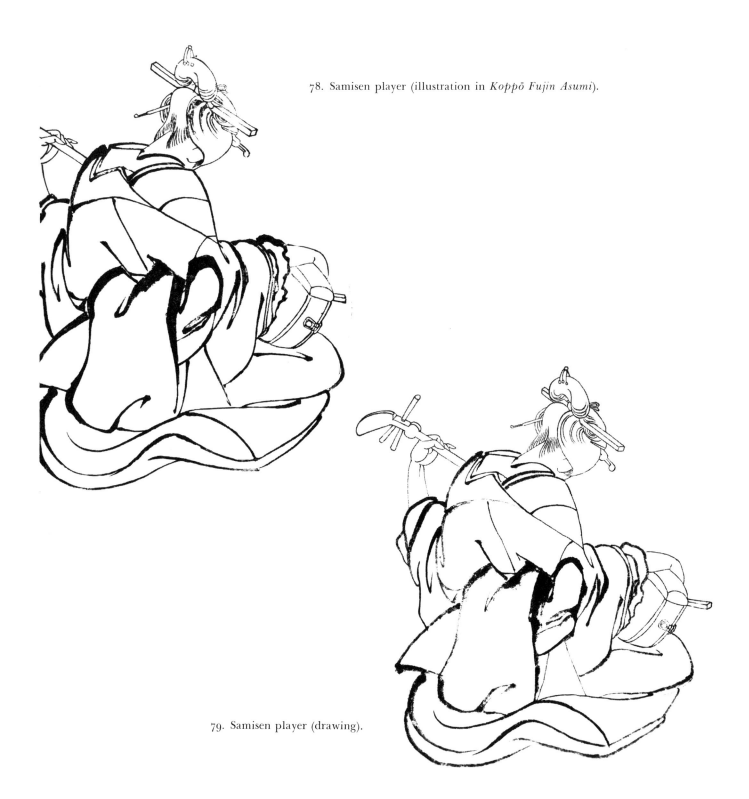

78. Samisen player (illustration in *Koppō Fujin Asumi*).

79. Samisen player (drawing).

80. Woman and octopus (rough sketch with *pentimenti*).

81. Woman and octopus (detail of print).

There is little evidence that Hokusai ever painted portraits. Self-portraits are likewise rarely found in his repertory, but numerous casual sketches show him, usually as an older man, in highly informal situations. They accord with what we take to be his actual portrait. One of the most appealing of these, done at the age of 62 or 63, has been greatly enlarged and reproduced as the frontispiece. It is ironically signed "Katsushika The Venerable." It is shown in its true proportions as well as in sharp contrast in a group of faces and bodies where the prevailing style is caricatural. There is no reason to suppose that when he was sketching or merely caricaturing individuals of all kinds he was not setting down authentic and recognizable people. Even in his obviously comic pictures, he shows himself a sharp physiognomist, and at his

frontispiece

figure 87

82. Boy with puppies.

83. Boy spinning top.

85. Seated boy.

清裕記又寄

五月廿日

86. "May 18" (drawing for *Nisshin-Joma-chō*).

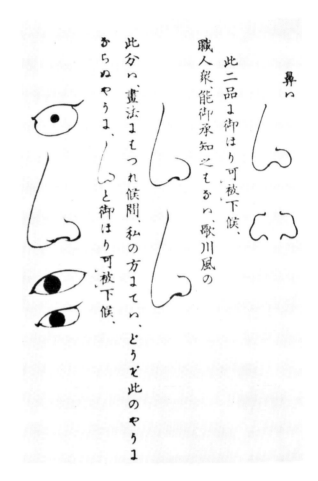

鼻口

此二品ま御はり可被下候、
職人衆、能御承知之るい、歌川風の
此分い、畫法まもつれ候間、私の方まてい、どうぞ此のやうま
あらぬやうま、〳〵と御はり可被下候、

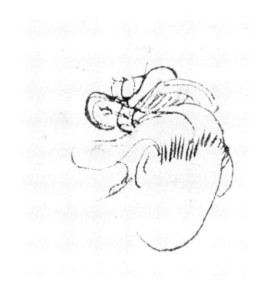

89. Face of Chinese lady.

90. Featureless woman's face.

91. Fragment of letter from Hokusai to his publishers.

88. Miscellaneous faces.

87. Miscellaneous faces and caricatures.

best he evinces great psychological insight. The group of sketches collected here are divided into those in which interest centers on form and features and those which stress character and personality; among the latter are included faces which derive from the human without necessarily being those of monsters.

We may introduce the discussion of Hokusai faces with a famous page composed of three women and one man, the latter in profile and the former in three-quarter view. The woman in the upper left, agreeably plump, carries her head as does the woman kneeling before her mirror in figure 74. The face on the upper right is un- doubtedly that of a courtesan, as evidenced by the tissue paper she holds in her mouth (a convention frequently observed in erotic prints). The third, in the lower right-hand corner, has a haughty quality, emphasized by the sharpness of the line, which relates it to the formal study of a woman wearing an elaborate floral head- dress which she is adjusting with her delicately drawn left hand. Both faces represent the type of aristocratic lady, usually Chinese, that Hokusai portrayed in illustrations of historical novels.

figure 88

figure 89

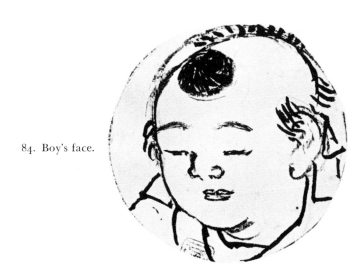

84. Boy's face.

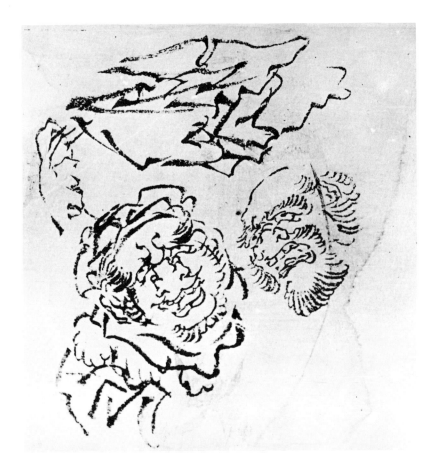

94. Two scowling faces.

93. Head of a demon.

95. Head of demon with animal features.

92. Head of a demon with human features.

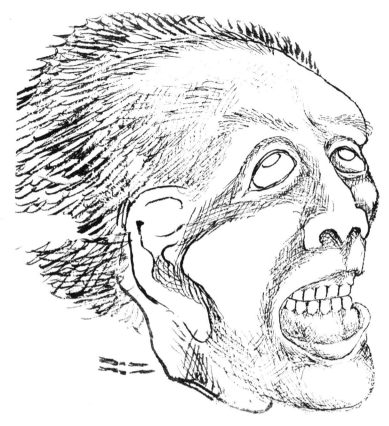

97. Spectral face.

96. Spectral face (water-color wash).

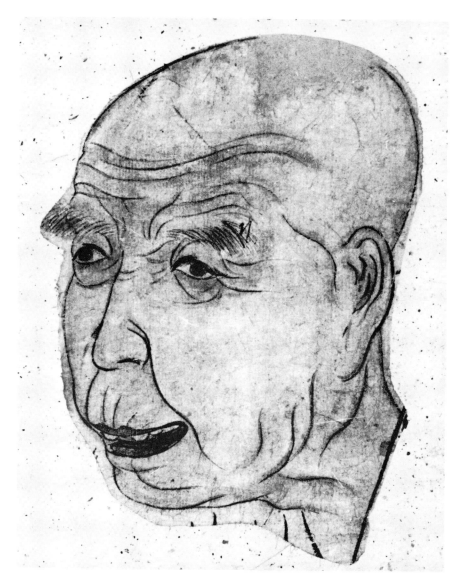

98. Man (or woman?) with shaven head (water-color wash).

The man in this group is clearly a worker or farmer; the sharpness of his nose in profile is typical, but it must be remarked that when the face is shown head-on the nose becomes squat and stubby, an inconsistency hard to explain.

That expressiveness is not dependent on details of features is *figure 90* shown by the little fragment of a woman's face in simple contour.

99. Ebisu seated.

104. Warriors at rest.

100. Daikoku astride a rat.

When he did begin to fill in, Hokusai was more conscious of the quality of the eyes and the nose than of the mouth. He states this explicitly in a letter of instructions, sent to his publishers for trans- *figure 91* mittal to his engravers. He wanted particularly to be true to life and to avoid the "Kuniyoshi look." He himself is not always con- sistent, as the man in the page just studied has a very peculiarly placed iris. *figures*

Next we have some fierce faces; whether demonic or human or *92 to 95* animal, they share a certain quality of maleness. A more unworldly *figure 96* pair of faces looks almost skeletal or spectral, the third one has a completely shaven head, bushy eyebrows, and a very long mouth *figure 97*

figure 98

over protruding teeth. The folds of the face and the volumes of the skull are indicated with chiaroscuro shadings—a technique seldom employed by Hokusai. The face is ambiguous as well as striking; it could be that of a woman. The shaven head is equally characteristic of a Buddhist nun or monk.

Hokusai frequently used the subject of the Seven Gods of Good Luck, especially Ebisu, Daikoku, and Hotei, the three most often associated with wealth and good cheer. Since they are popular deities he treats them with freedom and gusto, and he takes liberties with their iconography. Ebisu, for instance, is normally shown either in the act of fishing for the *tai*, or of holding it under his

figure 99

arm. Here is a variant showing EBISU SEATED on a bankside, his fishing basket to the right and wine jars to the left, obviously getting ready to eat the *tai* lying all prepared on the platter in front of him. Hokusai has transformed a standard representation of a traditional theme into a study of gormandizing.

In the drawing of Daikoku we see the god astride a huge rat—

figure 100

emblematic of wealth—which he is whipping with a very big carrot. To the left at the back a boy is sweeping the rat's droppings into a basket. (The combination of rat and carrot in connection with Daikoku is also used in *Manga* XII, but in a different and rather

figure 101

bawdy context.) The representation of Hotei in another drawing is very different in style and mood. He sits on a huge bag looking sober; a *koto* is stretched across his knees. This composition can be observed in *Santai Gafu* ("The Book of Painting in Three Forms") and elsewhere.

The Way of Romantic Realism: Heroes and Warriors

figure 102

Although little known because it is infrequently reproduced, Hokusai's drawing, "Saint George," has been one of the most highly praised of his depictions of martial subjects. The drawing passed from the hands of Hayashi to the famous collector Henri Vever; it is still in Paris in a private collection. Hayashi's seal is visible on the lower right; the calligraphic lines running lengthwise on the sheet are merely showing through the thin paper from the other side. Focillon waxes dithyrambic about this work. He

101. Hotei playing the *koto* (water-color wash).

103. Warriors on horseback (working drawing for the *Suikoden* series, with *pentimenti*).

102. Rider on rearing horse (rough drawing with many *pentimenti* and pasted-on corrections).

describes it as a *dessin de statuaire*, evidently seeing in it monumental qualities that elude other critics. If merited, that description would be a singular contradiction of Hokusai's special gifts as a draftsman, and in particular his superb control of line. Focillon implies that he was building up from the bottom the composition of the warrior astride a rearing horse, like a sculptor modeling in clay. If we compare this sketch with all other sketches we know, we must agree that the use of so many tentative strokes, both in red and in black, is very unusual. The subject is undoubtedly drawn from the *Shimpen Suiko Gwa Den;* he did many other representations of WARRIORS ON HORSEBACK, some of them engaged in an intricate form of dueling. I have not found any woodblock that corresponds exactly with the drawing. The pose is very much the same as that assigned to Sogō no Gōro, one of the martial figures in a series of prints by Kuniyoshi. The warrior in our drawing closely resembles Hokusai's standard models, however. In my opinion, the evidences of groping mean that the drawing was started by a pupil; the firm lines and refinements of detail found in the little pasted bits of paper, which show up as lighter areas, are undoubtedly corrections in the hand of the master. The Boston Museum owns another version of this drawing, undoubtedly by a pupil also. It may help throw some light on Hokusai's definitive intentions until the final version turns up.

By contrast with the tentative character of "Saint George," the superb sheet of the WARRIORS AT REST, a detail of which is shown in figure 11, should rank as one of Hokusai's masterpieces. The twenty-one martial personages are identifiable as members of the band in "One Hundred and Eight Heroes of the *Suikoden.*" They are shown here in a rare mood of serenity, quite unusual for such intensely active individuals. The format of this drawing suggests that it is part of a *makimono* or hand-scroll depicting the entire group. This, therefore, might be the first state, in the master's own hand, of the long scroll in the possession of the Freer Gallery. This unfinished work in which the painted sections are in vivid tones is more than likely the work of a follower who very cleverly copied the figures from the woodblocks and assembled them in a continuous composition. Whether Hokusai ever saw the work is open

figure 103

figure 104

figure 105

105. The Heroes of the *Suikoden* (fragment of painted scroll).

106. Crouching samurai (detail from a sheet of miscellaneous drawings, see figure 63).

to question, but we may accept it as a conscientious adaptation of his designs by a capable disciple.

Hokusai may have been somewhat fanciful in inventing Chinese figures, but there is no doubt that his rendering of Japanese heroes and men-at-arms shows evidence of careful study. The man kneeling before the squatting samurai, the ancient archer, and the two

figure 106

figure 107

107. Archer in medieval costume (drawing with color notations).

108. Shōki, the Demon Queller (drawing with *pentimenti*).

109. Shōki, the Demon Queller (water-color wash).

figure 108
figure 109
figure 110

studies of a man about to engage in duel are all products of sharp observation, either of the details of historic armor or of the poses and physical tensions inherent in the subject. When there is need to express more than mere energy, Hokusai will dramatize the mood by the use of short, jagged strokes of the brush, as in the BLACK TORNADO drawing. This represents a legendary pirate, named Kokusen, who strides forth to meet the enemy, making the very waves bend before the imperious fury of his approach.

Hokusai was not a bloodthirsty man, but he would not have been of his time and country had he not reveled in the sanguinary episodes of Japanese history. With no great difficulty one could collect a set of his illustrations under a heading such as "The Disasters of War" and confront them with some illustrious European counterparts. There would be as much horror, but the tone would be different. Goya's savagery would be missing, as would Callot's detachment and Breughel's macabre humor. He gave little to suggest pity for the victims, but neither did he gloat; rather, his drawings represent an appreciation of the fine points of warfare and a delight in their proper observance.

figure 111
figure 112
figure 113
figure 114

DECAPITATION of an enemy has been frequently portrayed in Japanese art, but never with as much gusto as in a detail shown in figure 9. The follow-through attitude of the executioner, with one foot on the neck of his victim and his glance directed at the flying head, invincibly suggests a parallel with a familiar sport. The GATHERING-UP OF HEADS depicted in the next drawing strikes a note halfway between some kind of harvesting and garbage-collecting—this, for once, is realism with a vengeance. Scenes of fighting in small boats occur frequently in the *Shimpen Suikoden*. The first drawing, with the winner shown with his back to us, has no particular merit other than that of being typical. Its companion piece is immensely more powerful in depicting the fierce intentness of the warrior rushing at his enemy. His momentum so carries him away that he almost follows his victim into the water. Incidentally, the lines of force indicating splashing water do not disappear in the woodcuts.

figure 115

THE ARREST OF KIDOMARU treats a violent subject taken at a moment of suspense. The bandit Kidomaru, having attempted to kill

黑旋風李逵

110. "Black Tornado."

111. Decapitation (detail from study sheet illustrated in figure 9).

黒旋風李逵

110. "Black Tornado."

111. Decapitation (detail from study sheet illustrated in figure 9).

112. A gathering-up of heads.

113. Fighter drowning two enemies from a boat.

Raiko Yorimitsu, is struggling against two of the latter's henchmen who are trying to tie him up. We are not certain that they will succeed; the bandit is still not disarmed and may yet escape. This is one of Hokusai's most closed and tightly-knit compositions. With its profusion of *pentimenti* in red and black it looks more confused than it actually is. There is a deliberateness, one might almost say stateliness, about the three men that suggests the theater: they seem to be consciously posing.

114. Fighter throwing an enemy into the water.

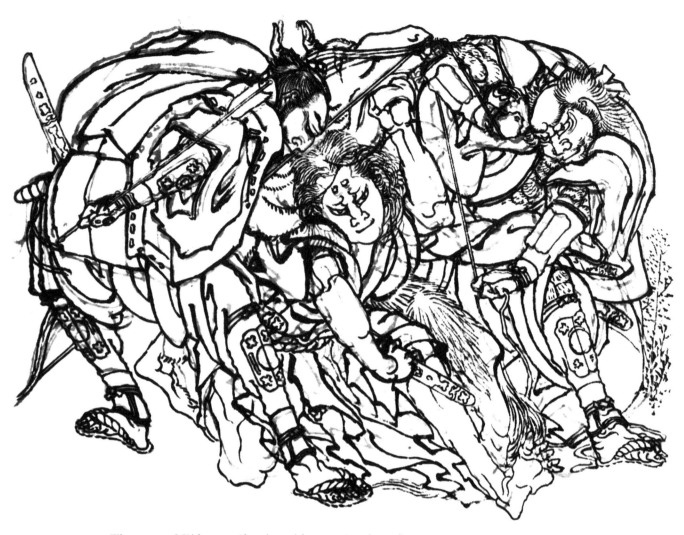

115. The arrest of Kidomaru (drawing with many *pentimenti*).

116. The Rape (drawing with *pentimenti*).

117. Illustration from *Shimpen Suiko Ga Den*.

figure 116

figure 117

An equal sense of deliberateness pervades another often described but rarely reproduced drawing, THE RAPE, which was formerly in the Vever Collection; its present whereabouts are unknown. Goncourt long ago identified it as a detail from a scene in the *Shimpen Suikoden*. It forms the right-hand portion of the scene in which Sokō, the leader of the One Hundred and Eight Heroes, arrives in time to save the Lady Fujiyo from "danger." Here also the pattern of the over-all design is closed—the four hands of the protagonists provide most of the dramatic tension. Again we have a moment of suspended animation, and the theatricalism of the situation is heightened by the lack of facial expression among the protagonists. There is a copy of this drawing, obviously by a weaker hand, in the Boston Museum.

HOKUSAI AS TEACHER

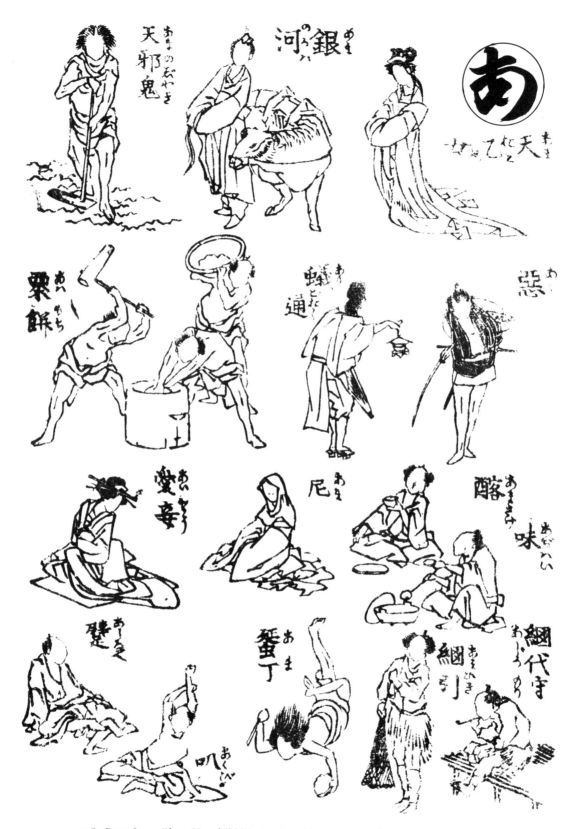

128. Page from *Ehon Hayabiki* illustrating thirteen words beginning with the sound "ah."

THREE Though he disliked formal teaching, Hokusai had a strongly developed pedagogical instinct. Many of his works, and in particular that collection of miscellaneous sketches enriched with a profusion of subjects, the *Manga*, were produced to meet a pressing demand for examples of his art. The apparent desire of the public to copy his pictures was also encouraged by the publication of several "how-to-do-it" manuals of drawing and painting by Hokusai. Goncourt and later critics have described these books, but without deriving many conclusions from them. The tendency has been to regard them as potboilers or, in some cases, as simple exercises in virtuosity. While they may not have as much merit as, for instance, Klee's *Pedagogical Sketch-book*, they are useful: they provide clues to Hokusai's own methods and basic point of view, and they are also, conceivably, in their technical rationalization, an indication of how he trained his own pupils.

Like any virtuoso who is prevailed upon to impart his secrets, Hokusai knew that his readiness to oblige was not so much a tribute to his generosity as proof that he was not giving anything essential away. He always warned his public that while drawing was easy enough, nothing much could ever be gained by imitating his or anybody else's technique. A slavish adherence to rules leads nowhere. Nature is the best teacher, and an individual should follow his own inspiration. These principles recur constantly in his prefaces, his correspondence, and his reported conversations. We surmise that he preached them to his amanuenses. Acquiring the

118. Frontispiece to v. 2 of *Ryakuga Haya Oshie*.

manual skill to approximate one or another of his manners was not too arduous; far more important was to see as the master did, and to be able to grasp the essential character of the thing seen. We must assume therefore that the most valuable aspect of his teaching lay in his oral comments rather than in the occasional firming up of a line or checking the accuracy with which a recipe was being applied or a model followed.

Hokusai's explicit teachings fall into two categories—precepts and examples—and may be conveniently described in that sequence. We are immediately struck by his refusal to set these precepts forth as original; the traditions of both the Tosa and the Kano painters are evoked, and ultimately the classic canons of Chinese art. Though his *Ryakuga Haya Oshie*, or "Method for Learning Rapid Drawing" is prefaced by the picture of an artist working with five brushes, one in each hand, one in the mouth and held by each

figure 118

foot—a clear allusion to his own reputation for indulging in spec-
tacular tricks—it closes with a demonstration of how the brush   *figure 119*
should be held to obtain specific effects. These techniques have
remained unchanged for centuries.

Volume 2 of the *Ryakuga* is devoted to helping the learner
evolve pictorial forms out of calligraphic pictograms. The earlier   *figure 120*
examples, such as the FISHERMAN, seem uncomplex, while later
ones, such as the THREE SAGES DISPORTING THEMSELVES ON A MOUN-   *figure 121*
TAIN, appear to be somewhat more involved; and greater freedom
and boldness occur as we progress. The instance of THE MIRROR-   *figure 122*
POLISHER, especially appealing because of its allusion to Hokusai's
family background, serves to make the point that the learner, after
carefully studying the lessons of the past masters and making sure
that he understands them, is strongly encouraged to trust his imagination. In the example of the *Keisai* or BEAUTIFUL COURTESAN, he   *figure 123*
states that "although the letters are to be transformed drastically,
the spirit of the drawing is not to be distorted," and he points out
that the character for *makura* (which is the knot into which the

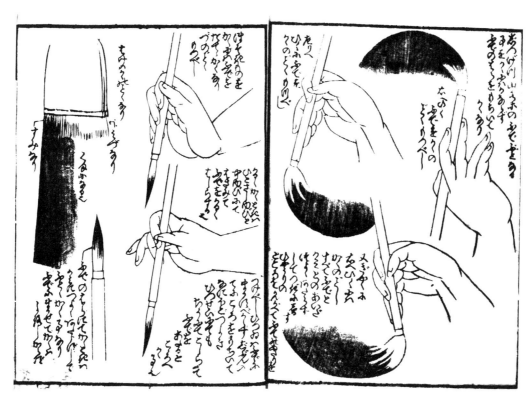

119. How to hold the brush (illustration).

obi is tied and which the courtesan is required to wear in front) can be combined with the character meaning man into a visual pun so that he appears to be lying on it. *Makura* also means "pillow," which rounds out the pun.

Exploiting the visual, auditory, and associative aspects of forms is characteristic of the Tosa School; very often their paintings involve the participation of a group of artists in a series of games requiring not only skill with the brush but familiarity with poetry. This cultural pastime, implying a high degree of intellectual attainment, was not beyond the grasp of Hokusai. Theoretically debarred by virtue of his social rank from the advantages of a classical education, he gives every evidence of having been a literate man. Without introducing concepts that might distort the meaning of Japanese sociological history, one might say that he was one of the agents of that egalitarian process which began before the nineteenth century. There was no reason why the middle and lower classes should not enjoy esoteric cultural pleasures hitherto considered the privilege of a minority; our artist does not hesitate to use the popular medium of the print to treat subjects hitherto rendered exclusively in paintings. (Hillier's *Hokusai*, Plate V, has an excellent reproduction of one such print.)

A sequel to *Ryakuga*, called *Haya Shinan* ("Book of Quick Sketching," 1834) stresses another classical precept especially dear *figure 124* to the adherents of the Kano School. The painter must ascertain the natural and logical relationships of forms one with the other: *figure 125* organic phenomena such as trees, plants, and flowers have a specific order of growth; arrangement in landscapes and the components thereof are guided by proportion and distance, human activity by inner significance and perhaps protocol. Basically this means that there is a specific order of brush strokes, and a precise calculation of the amount of ink to be carried and the pressure to be applied. Strict adherence to this rule is of course sterile; it merely provides the means of recording the results of careful observation. As usual, the student is urged not to confuse means with ends.

It is in volume 1 of *Ryakuga* that we note a curious disavowal of a basic Chinese canon and the substitution of a formula of utterly alien provenance. In the preface Hokusai is quoted as

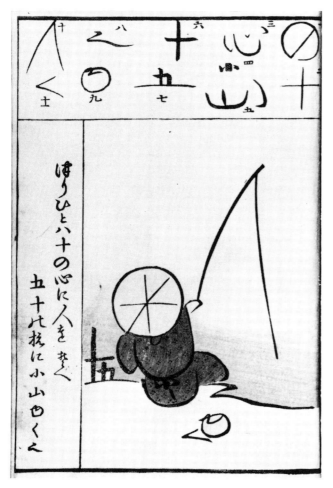

120. A fisherman, built up from simple ideograms, which compose the poem on the left. (The starting characters are *jugo* or "fifteen.")

121. Three sages disporting themselves on a mountain. (The starting character is *yama* or "mountain".)

やとをゆびらのふ
よとふくるり
その のむ

122. The mirror polisher. (The character interpreted is
kagami-ya.)

deriding that most ancient tenet, *ten-chi-jin,* which sets the correct
relationship of man to mountain to heaven as one to ten to one
hundred. "The proper scale of things, he states, is learned only
through wielding a ruler and a pair of dividers. Well-executed cir-
cles and straight lines will lead to a fine and delicate draftsman-
ship."[16] To illustrate his meaning he presents a series of forms of
all kinds, first in the standard manner, then in the new mechanical
fashion. There is no doubt that as far as geometrical analysis goes
these diagrams are very ingenious. However, the proportions un-
covered by the schemata seem to be based on actual observation of
forms: the ox or bull or traveler in the snow is drawn first, and not
the geometric forms, which consequently must be arbitrary. We
seem to have here a rudimentary kind of cubism *avant la lettre;* the

figure 126

123. The Beautiful Courtesan. (The character interpreted is *makura*.)

cone and the cube are missing but volume is obviously easy to convey through the juxtaposition of curving lines.

Some have tried to compare these diagrams with the stereometric diagrams found in the *Sketchbook* of Villard de Honnecourt, but there is no valid basis for that comparison. Some pages in Hokusai's book do come close to Villard, as in the page analyzing insects. His grasshopper is similar to the medieval architect's, but there is really little evidence from which a parallel could be drawn between Hokusai and Villard. About all they have in common is the recommendation to the student: ponder the example carefully and avoid using the formula until you have completely understood it. It is far more likely that Hokusai saw, either at first hand or through a version copied by a fellow artist such as Masayo-

figure 127

shi, some plates from Van de Passe's *Encyclopedia*, "The Light of Painting and Drawing" (Amsterdam, 1643). Here are diagrams of animals done with ruler and compass, similar to Hokusai's. But Hokusai could not possibly have grasped the Euclidean implications of the formulae, and was not too serious about their acceptance. There is not much evidence that he used them in his own work except that, having once seen these grids, the onlooker is irresistibly led to apply them mentally every time he encounters familiar forms in the artist's prints. What this excursus really indicates is an open mind on the artist's part and a readiness to experiment.

124. Man riding a lion, with an analysis of the order of the brush strokes.

Among the other manuals the most interesting ones are exemplars: *Ehon Hayabiki*, *Santai Gafu*, and *Ippitsu Gafu*. *Ehon Hayabiki* is a kind of pictographic dictionary in which each of the forty-nine sounds of the *hiragana* syllabary, represented by a distinct character, starts a set of given words, all of them illustrated. One page may therefore have from six to a dozen different subjects in compositions using one or several figures, both human and animal. In all cases, since each composition uses at most two inches of page space, characteristic attitude and gesture become more important than facial expression, and all faces are blank. As far as I can make out there is no attempt at weaving the calligraphic symbol into the pattern of the drawing, as was done in *Ryakuga* (cf. the MIRROR MAKER, figure 122); here the auditory association is arbitrary.

figure 128

125. Horses, with an analysis of the order of the brush strokes.

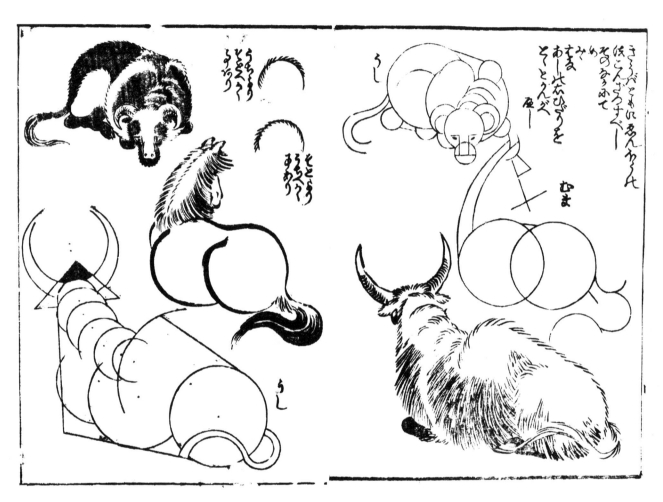

126. Stereometric elaboration of various animals (double-page illustration).

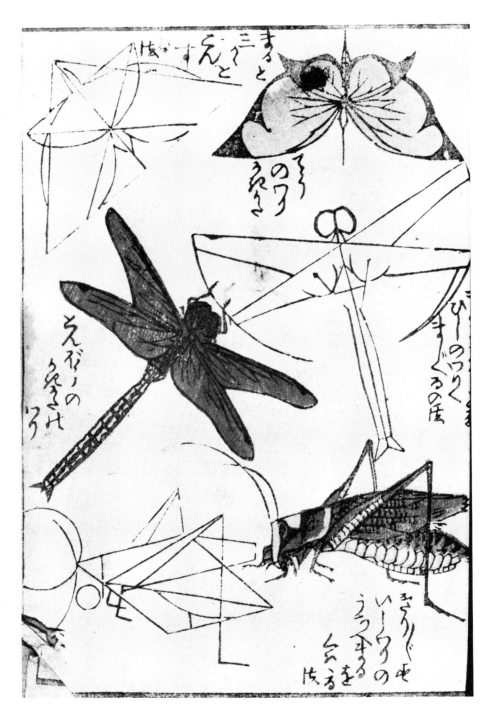

127. Stereometric elaboration of various insects (illustration).

b) Three drunkards

c) Three goats

opposite and above: 129. Three illustrations from *Santai Gafu.*

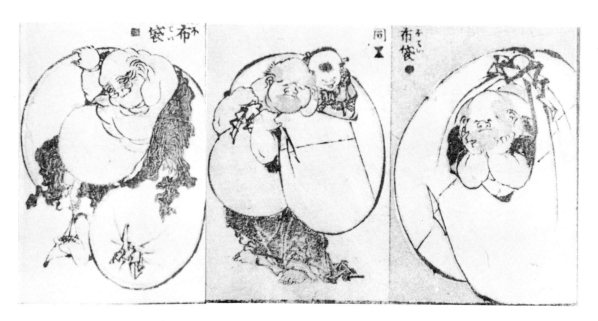

a) The God Hotei

figure 129

"The Book of Drawing by Three Methods," or *Santai Gafu,* is introduced with two slightly varying interpretations: "He who cannot stand cannot walk and he who cannot walk cannot run. Now, to stand is *shin* (that is, to copy faithfully); to walk is *gyō* (freely rendered, to portray imaginatively); to run is *sō* (or to dash off a rapid sketch). This is how I would classify the productions of pictorial art." Elsewhere Hokusai expresses himself as follows: "In calligraphy there are three forms; but it is not only in calligraphy that these forms exist, it is in everything that man observes. Thus, when a flower begins to bloom, its form is, so to speak, rigid *(shin)*; when the flower fades, the form is as if neglected *(gyō)*; when it falls to earth, the form is as if abandoned and disorderly *(sō)*." Provided one does not take the metaphors[17] too literally, it is not too difficult to reconcile both interpretations by examining the compositions in *Santai Gafu.* These always come in sets of three, whether together in a single frame or in three separate ones. *Shin* is indicated by a black square, *gyō* by a round dot, and *sō* by inverted triangles. Esoteric implications are beyond the ordinary Western viewer: I cannot see in these pictures anything other than the treatment of subjects from three different angles; the points of view are physical rather than intellectual. Where they are all within one frame, the sum of the parts is greater than one would expect, as there is the added value of ingenious composition.

figure 130

Ippitsu Gafu, or "Book of Paintings in One Brush-stroke," is, like *Ehon Hayabiki,* filled with tiny figures and scenes executed in a manner which recalls that of the *son filé* of a string instrument. The artist does not in either case lift his tool—bow or brush—while proceeding; he produces effects by twisting its position and varying the intensity of his pressure; the painter, however, is striving for rapidity rather than for retardation and when he is through he has made a complete statement in terms that combine utmost economy with fluid elegance. What may have started as a game for the purpose of displaying virtuosity ends by being a vehicle for Hokusai's supreme object-lesson: control of the line to express form.

130. Strong men and wrestlers (illustration).

NOTES

SELECTIVE BIBLIOGRAPHY

INDEX

1. Tadamasa Hayashi (1853–1906) settled in Paris in the 1880's and began importing Japanese works of art, especially prints. His shop, according to Edmond de Goncourt, became so exclusive that one could enter it only by appointment. Hayashi assisted Goncourt in the preparation of his books on Hokusai and Utamaro. Samuel Bing (1838–1905) was German-born but also settled in Paris as a dealer. As a promotor of the *Art Nouveau* movement he influenced its adoption of Japanese ornamental style.

2. O. E. Holloway, *The Graphic Art of Japan; the Classical School.* London, Alec Tiranti, 1957; pp. 20–22.

3. Michel Revon was a French jurist who was attached to the Japanese Ministry of Justice. The University of Paris conferred a doctorate on him on the basis of a remarkably thorough monograph on Hokusai (see Bibliography).

4. Hillier's studies on Hokusai and his followers, partially published in *Connoisseur* since 1956, are the subject of a forthcoming book.

5. Jakob Rosenberg, *Rembrandt the Draughtsman, with Consideration of the Problem of Authenticity.* Fogg Museum of Art, Harvard University, n.d. (Reprinted from *Daedalus*, vol. 86, no. 2, September, 1956.)

6. E. F. Fenollosa, *Special Exhibitions of the Pictorial Art of Japan and China*, vol. 1.

7. The first twelve books of the *Manga* were published between 1814 and 1834. Volume XIII was issued in 1850, one year following Hokusai's death. It is presumed that he had not edited it. Volumes XIV and XV came out in 1875 and 1878 respectively.

9. The term was coined by T. Voelker, who called his study the *Ukiyoe Quartet* (Leiden, Brill, 1949).

10. B. H. Chamberlain, *Things Japanese,* 4th edition (London, 1902), p. 436.

11. One added reason for thinking that the Metropolitan Museum drawing

is a study for a painting is its size, which is much larger than the usual sketch for prints or book illustrations.

12. The Paris and the London versions differ very slightly in size, and the latter is a slightly more refined statement. The probability is that they are both by Hokusai. Each drawing has the dancing poet on the right and two squatting men on the upper right, but the crouching woman of the London version is replaced by the Seller of New Year's Poems in the other sketch. The dimensions of both are approximately h. 11″, w. 15½″.

13. Reproduced in Hillier's *Hokusai,* figure 80.

14. The name Sōri seems to have been used by five different artists, including Hokusai, who adopted it between 1796 and 1802.

15. Adapted from Goncourt's *Hokousaï* (p. 142 of the definitive edition, n.d.).

16. *Ibid,* p. 200.

17. See Lucy Driscoll and K. Toda, *Chinese Calligraphy,* Chicago, 1935.

SELECTIVE BIBLIOGRAPHY

GENERAL STUDIES

Iijima, Hanjuro. *Katsushika Hokusai den*. Tokyo, 1893.

Goncourt, Edmond de. *Hokusaï*. Paris, 1895.

Revon, Michel. *Stude sur Hoksaï*. Paris, 1896.

Focillon, Henri. *Hokousai*. Paris, 1914.

Hillier, Jack R. *Hokusai; Paintings, Drawings and Woodcuts*. London, 1955.

Narazaki, M., and Yamaioto, K. *Hokusai*. Tokyo, 1958.

SPECIAL STUDIES

Dickens, F. W. *The Mangwa of Hokusai*. London, Transactions and Proceedings of the Japan Society, 1901–1904 and 1906.

Rothenstein, W. *Two Drawings by Hok'sai*. Broad Campden, 1910.

Loewenstein, F. E. *Die Handzeichnungen der Japanischen Holzschnittmeister*. Plauen im Vogtland, 1922.

Nagasse, T. *La Figure Humaine dans les Estampes Japonaises*. Paris, 1934.

Inouye, K. *The Fragments of the Study of Hokusai*. Tokyo, Ukiyoyeshi, 1929.

Kubota, Jean K. "The *Mangwa* books of Hokusai." Unpublished Master's thesis, State University of Iowa, 1954.

Hillier, J. R. "Hokusai; some drawings and problems of attribution," *Connoisseur*, 137 (May, 1956), 167–74.

————, "Drawings by Hokusai's followers: Taitō and Hokkei," *Connoisseur*, 139 (May–June, 1957), 157–61 and 232–33.

————, "Hokusai drawings in the Harari Collection," *Connoisseur*, 145 (June, 1960), 17–21.

Bowie, Theodore. "Hokusai and the comic tradition in Japanese painting," *College Art Journal*, xix, 3 (Spring, 1960), 210–24.

REPRODUCTIONS OF WORKS BY HOKUSAI

Day and Night in the Four Seasons, Sketches by Hokusai. Boston, Museum of Fine Arts, 1957.

The Hokusai Sketchbooks, Selections from the MANGA. James A. Michener, editor. Tokyo, 1958.

Fugaku hiyaku-kei: One hundred views of Fuji. With an Introduction by J. Hillier and description of the plates by F. W. Dickins, New York, 1958.

Hokusaï, un Maître de l'Estampe Japonaise. Willy Boller, editor. Lausanne, 1955.

Hokusai. With an Introduction by Joe Hloucha. Prague, n.d.

For descriptions of the original books illustrated by Hokusai and mentioned in the text, see K. Toda, *Descriptive Catalogue of Japanese and Chinese Illustrated Books,* Chicago, 1931.

CATALOGUES OF SPECIAL EXHIBITIONS

Fenollosa, E. F. *Special Exhibitions of the Pictorial Art of Japan and China: Vol. 1, Hokusai and his School.* Boston, Museum of Fine Arts, 1893.

————, *The Masters of Ukioye . . . as shown in Exhibition at the Fine Arts Building.* New York, 1896.

————, *Catalogue of the Exhibition of Paintings by Hokusai.* Tokyo, 1900.

Hayashi, T. *Dessins, estampes, livres illustrés du Japon.* Paris, 1902.

British Museum. *The Work of Hokusai.* London, 1948.

Stedelijk Museum. *Rembrandt, Hokusai, Van Gogh.* Amsterdam, 1951.

Arts Council of Great Britain. *Hokusai Drawings and Water-colours.* 1954.

Kunsthalle Recklinghausen. *Hokusai-Mataré.* Recklinghausen, 1956.

Stedelijk-Van Abbe Museum. *Hokusai.* Eindhoven, 1956.

Galerie Huguette Berès. *Hokusai.* Paris, 1958.

Freer Gallery of Art. *Selected Works by Katsushika Hokusai.* Washington, 1960.

INDEX